Introducing Contemporary Feminist Thought

Introducing Contemporary Feminist Thought

Mary Evans

Polity Press

Copyright © Mary Evans 1997

The right of Mary Evans to be identified as author of this work has been asserted in accordance with the Copyright, Designs and Patents Act 1988.

First published in 1997 by Polity Press in association with Blackwell Publishers Ltd.

2 4 6 8 10 9 7 5 3 1

Editorial office:
Polity Press
65 Bridge Street
Cambridge CB2 1UR, UK

Marketing and production:
Blackwell Publishers Ltd
108 Cowley Road
Oxford OX4 1JF, UK

Published in the USA by
Blackwell Publishers Inc.
Commerce Place
350 Main Street
Malden, MA 02148, USA

ISBN 0-7456-1475-2
ISBN 0-7456-1476-0 (pbk)

A CIP catalogue record for this book is available from the British Library.

Library of Congress Cataloging-in-Publication Data

Evans, Mary, 1946–
 Introducing contemporary feminist thought / Mary Evans.
  p. cm.
 Includes bibliographical references and index.
 ISBN 0-7456-1475-2. — ISBN 0-7456-1476-0
 1. Feminist theory. I. Title
HQ1190.E92 1997   97–559
305.42'01–dc21   CIP

Typeset in 11 on 13 pt Sabon
by Wearset, Boldon, Tyne and Wear.
Printed in Great Britain by Hartnolls Ltd, Bodmin, Cornwall.

This book is printed on acid-free paper.

Contents

Acknowledgements		vi
Introduction		1
1	Enter Women	4
2	Public and Private: Women and the State	24
3	Engendering Knowledge	44
4	Representation	65
5	The Body	85
6	Feminism and the Academy	106
7	Worlds of Difference?	123
Notes		139
Bibliography		149
Index		163

Acknowledgements

I was fortunate to receive a great deal of help from other people in writing this book and preparing it for publication. Andrew Winnard and Pamela Thomas at Polity were helpful and sympathetic editors. Sue Sherwood and Carole Davis were endlessly patient with revisions to the text, and from Pat Macpherson, Jan Montefiore, Anne Seller, Mary McIntosh and Janet Sayers I received careful and critical advice. I am deeply grateful to all of them.

Introduction

The focus of this book is, as the title indicates, contemporary feminism. But the account of feminism presented here is explicitly that of a feminism with close, not to say fundamental, links to the academy and the academic 'form' of feminism, 'Women's Studies'. As such the book is not about Women's Studies, but in many cases readers will recognize issues and themes that are common currency in Women's Studies courses. Contemporary feminism, particularly in the West, is very much a creature with important academic roots. Indeed, one of the many freedoms that feminism has helped to create is the sense of the legitimacy of explicitly personal and subjective material within the academy. It was not, as many feminists have pointed out, that the personal and the subjective were not features of the academy, but they were often disguised as 'objectivity' and the 'real facts'. These apparently objective truths were objective in so far as they were constructed and legitimated by the most powerful group within the Western academy, a group that it is impossible to describe in any terms other than white, male and middle class. So powerful was the hold of this section of the population on teaching and research in higher education that different views and experiences,

1

particularly and crucially views and experiences from outside that group, were seldom, if ever, given space or credence.

But while saying this, what has to be said at the same time, and said emphatically, is that whilst this dominant culture was in many ways exclusive and narrow, it also contained its own dissent, difference and distinction. It is thus that in engagement with the intellectual past there is a constant need both to maintain scepticism about its judgements and retain respect for its achievements. Equally, we have to develop new ways of discussing and debating the central issues of our culture. 'The master's tools', wrote Audré Lorde in one of the best-known feminist interventions about the academy, 'will never dismantle the master's house'. And as she went on to say, 'this fact is only threatening to those women who still define the master's house as their only source of support'.[1]

Those 'master's tools' to which Audré Lorde referred are a constant, if sometimes hidden, feature of the following pages. It was with inspiration from Marx, Freud and Foucault (amongst others) that feminists constructed radical re-readings and re-interpretations of our social and emotional worlds. Yet at the same time, and crucially, no engagement with these figures would have occurred if diverse women, from Simone de Beauvoir to Audré Lorde, had not resisted and rejected the nature of the master's house that those theoretical tools had constructed. Here, therefore, is the suggestion that the master's tools *have* been used to good effect by feminists, and that dialogue and debate with post-Enlightenment political and social theory is a central element of contemporary feminism.[2] But, at the same time, two provisos remain: the first is that the figures who have been most inspirational to feminism have been figures from traditions of dissent in Western culture. The triumvirate mentioned above all stood, in various ways, for a rejection of bourgeois, conventional thought. Their radicalism may not have contained a radicalism about relations between women and men, but at the same time it contained a vision of human emancipation and human equality that remains important to this day. For those millions of women whose lives are curtailed and blighted by the incessant greed of global capitalism and its voracious demands for low paid labour,

Marx's critique of capitalism remains relevant. Indeed, the importance of retaining a knowledge of the *dynamic* of class relations in capitalism needs stressing in a culture that increasingly emphasizes identities of consumption rather than production.

So the intellectual past should not sit like a dead weight on our shoulders, but should be used – with scepticism and even irreverence – to understand the present. It is in resisting the authority of the academy that feminism has shown itself to be powerful, and in the further demonstration that the master's house is often not worth defending. Carole Pateman has pointed out 'the sexual contract' that lies at the heart of Western ideas of citizenship, just as Sasha Roseneil has documented the possibilities of feminist political action.[3] Both writers, and others working in the same tradition of non-complicity with the academic past, have illuminated the ways in which understanding informs and strengthens action. The purpose of this book is to suggest some of the main ways in which a feminist understanding of the world can disturb and disrupt conventional assumptions. Those 'conventional assumptions' may, in some cases, be apparently academic or theoretical, but a premise of the discussion here is that the boundaries between the academic/theoretical and the 'real' world are not firm and fixed. On the contrary, 'higher knowledge' is a major force in the organization of our daily, routine lives. Whilst we may not always recognize the origin or the meaning of the imperatives that we follow, they are a crucial part of our lives.

It should therefore be apparent that what is questioned in the literature reviewed here is the tradition of universalistic assumptions in the West. Indeed, it is a central thesis of the pages that follow that knowledge is deeply gendered, in terms of both who produces it and – more significantly – what is produced. It is not that there is women's knowledge and men's knowledge, as earlier feminist accounts of intellectual life have suggested, but that gendered assumptions are inter-woven into the fabric of our culture. Unpicking the strands of gendered bias is thus a crucial task for feminists: what follows is hopefully a guide to the ways in which the manifest inadequacies of what has so far passed for universal knowledge might be rejected in favour of more truly representative accounts of the world.

1
Enter Women

Let me begin this book with an autobiographical comment: when I went to university in 1964 there was no such thing as an explicitly feminist presence. Indeed, there were not very many women in universities, let alone women teaching a subject explicitly and unreservedly about women. At my *alma mater* (the London School of Economics) there were about eight male undergraduates for every female, and to say that the culture was vigorously masculine would be no exaggeration. The politics, the economics and the sociology that I was taught were all about the public world and the world of men. It simply did not occur to anyone, myself included, that it might be important to consider questions of gender in our discussions. Women, when they were mentioned at all, had a poor academic press from my left-wing (or at least Labour-voting) teachers, since women, it was stated, were more likely to vote Conservative than men. In those days of the white hot heat of Harold Wilson's Technological Revolution, anyone who stood in the way of the achievement of a meritocratic and technocratic social democracy was not to be trusted.

But women were as essential to young (and old) men in 1964 as they have ever been, and just as women barely appeared in the academic curriculum, so they were central to non-academic discussions. In the early 1960s, the rules of sexual relationships were being re-written, and my generation grew older within a set of shifting ideas about sexual behaviour. The Pill had just begun to be widely available, and widely discussed, and thus to a young, cosmopolitan cohort of students, it really did appear as if sexual intercourse, together with the Beatles, had been invented in 1964. Philip Larkin's ironic, and wry, poem about the changing moral climate of the 1960s ('Sexual intercourse began/In nineteen sixty-three')[1] caught some of the atmosphere of the time; what it left out was the resistance of women to the male construction of the new standards and the sheer confusion of the time, as differences of generation became politicized in a way unique to the post-war world. Into this mêlée older voices occasionally intervened; I remember the famous Agony Aunt Evelyn Home sweeping all before her in a vivid denunciation of sexual liberalization as defined by men. Faced with an audience almost exclusively made up of young men, determined to mock this determined advocate of pre-marital chastity, Evelyn Home argued a case for women that was seldom heard in the portals of our lecture theatres.

However persuasive her oratory, Evelyn Home could not change or prevent the shifts in ideas – and, of course, in behaviour – that took place in the following decade. Sex and sexuality became an explicit part of the agenda of the West, and by 1970 the rules and expectations that had governed the early 1960s had either disappeared or begun to disappear. As numerous histories of the 1960s have pointed out, by the end of the decade sexual codes had changed, 'permissiveness' had arrived and the explicit discussion of sexuality had become part of the *lingua franca* of the West.[2] Inevitably, a generation grew up believing that it had invented sex and, as firmly, believing that the past had been one long dark history of the repression of sexuality. Sexual 'freedom', the sexually explicit and sexual availability became synonymous with an expectation of personal liberation and the pursuit of individual happiness. Older voices (on all sides of the political spectrum) could point out that having heterosexual sex was nothing particularly novel and offered as much a lack of freedom as it did the promise of freedom, but these voices were often dismissed as 'Puritan', or even worse 'up-tight'.

This re-invention of sexuality took place, for the West, within the context of political systems still dominated by East–West rivalry and a fear of the threat of Soviet Communism as great as any in the 1950s. Indeed, one essential and salient point about the 1960s is that the national and inter-national politics of the decade, rather than the politics of inter-personal relations, were still locked into the dynamic of the early twentieth century and the West's terror of Communism. What brought the political and the personal together for many in the 1960s was the polarization of political opinion about the intervention of the United States in Vietnam. On the one hand, the 1960s had seen the rapid de-colonization of the old Western empires, whilst on the other, the world's major power carried out a massive, and essentially imper-ial, engagement in a non-Western country. The political legitimacy of the West, which had been saved by the victory over German fascism, now came under fire for its own authoritarianism, and, as some commentators saw it, its own version of fascism.[3]

The question of Vietnam thus became a rallying cry for a gen-eration, just as the Spanish Civil War had been a focus in the 1930s. Because the United States had become *the* power of the West in the years after 1945, its politics became the dominating factor for all its allies. But since Vietnam was not the only issue which beset the United States in the 1960s, other questions – par-ticularly about race and sexuality – rapidly became internation-ally significant. The Civil Rights movement in the United States dramatized relations between races in a way previously unknown in the post-war years, whilst the Black Power movement that developed from the struggle for civil rights transformed Western thinking about the construction of racial identities. The politics of the 1960s were dominated by confrontational issues, in which the ideological hegemony of the United States was shattered by internal and external opposition. As the North Vietnamese, the Black Panthers and the student revolutionaries of 1968 pointed out, the military power of the United States might be absolute, but that still left a great deal to discuss and negotiate about the order and the agenda of the social world.[4]

These turbulent politics, and this stormy decade, left its mark on countries and governments just as assuredly as it made, and often un-made individual lives. For once, the Western academy was intimately and directly involved in these political upheavals. Campuses across the United States were the sites of organized protest about government policy in Vietnam whilst European universities, particularly in France, gave rise to the resurgence of highly critical accounts of government policies. The definitive European case remains that of the Sorbonne, where the domestic arrangements (that is male access to the accommodation of female students) of a new campus at Nanterre became the point of contention that brought a government to crisis and threatened the stability of a whole society. Thus did sex and politics in the 1960s join together to form an explosive mix that radically de-stabilized both social institutions and social assumptions. The 'new' interpretation of the world in 1968 was *for* political and sexual liberation and *against* the war in Vietnam. A counter-culture, which at any other time might have been simply a shift in the behaviour of a generation, acquired not just a political meaning but also a real political power.

Into these events, and within these events, came a further current which arguably has had a more important *long-term* impact on social life than the protest movements of the 1960s. The current was that of feminism, and the claim by women for their right to self-determination and personal autonomy. It was, like any social movement, complicated and often contradictory, riddled with dissent and fired with messianic zeal. Feminism was in no sense 'new' to the twentieth century, but it assumed, in the 1960s and the 1970s, a new urgency and a new radicalism that made it a product of its times. If every generation has to re-invent the wheel – or tends to believe that it has just invented the wheel – so feminism in the West in the 1960s and 1970s took some time before it recognized its history and the longevity of the struggle that it represented.

The history of the 'resurgence' of feminism (as it is often described) in the 1960s has now been fully documented both in fiction and non-fiction. Of all the accounts written of the coming of feminism and the coming to feminism of a new generation,

7

one of the most vivid about the United States is Sara Davidson's *Loose Change*, which captures both some of the excitement and the chaos (whether sexual or intellectual) of the time.[5] But to identify that novel as a representative account of second wave feminism carries with it a set of assumptions about feminism, which requires immediate comment. The novel is set in the United States, and is about white, middle-class women who came to feminism through and within the academy. It is not about the world, and worlds, outside that assumptive world, and indeed the novel ends on a note of integration: the characters, having made their protests and lived their lives of adolescent rebellion, become re-integrated into a white, professionally successful, middle-class world.

What has to be recognized, and the point of introducing this novel into a discussion about feminism, is that feminism was always, and is still, a form of protest by women about their exclusion from full citizenship in Western, bourgeois society. Western, post-Enlightenment feminism essentially took issue with the construction of citizenship by that world – a form of citizenship that originally (and still to a certain extent today) excluded women, not necessarily through conscious intention or conscious decision, but through the non-thinking assumption that the people in the public world were all male. Indeed, in many situations and many contexts the term 'people' has actually been interpreted as exclusively male. Thus, from the beginning of the nineteenth century, the dominant (although by no means the only) tradition within feminism was one that fought for the extension to women of those rights (for example the vote and access to the professions and higher education) automatically enjoyed by men. Yet even in saying this, what requires comment is that the men with whom women are comparing themselves are white and middle class. No feminist campaigned for entry to the world of the relatively under-privileged manual worker, anymore than the point of comparison in feminist campaigns in the West were the disenfranchised and racial minorities. In her work on the 'hidden' feminism of working-class women, the British historian Sheila Rowbotham has reminded us that working-class women have a long history of campaigning for their rights (particularly for

Trade Union representation and equal workplace rights), but the thrust of her long and distinguished work has been to make the point that, in talking about feminism, we must be aware of its complexity and its different meaning for women in different classes and countries.[6]

Thus the first point we have to establish in a discussion of feminism is that the term 'feminism' in the 1990s needs more careful consideration than it received in the heady days of the late 1960s and early 1970s. Feminism has become more complex in its traditions, and the very word now demands a measure of deconstruction if we are ever to tease out from it the various appeals that this diverse movement makes to different constituencies. But the very diversity of feminism's appeal has given to it much of its creative energy; a movement that has always had both furious disputes and rock-solid agreements is one that allows difference and debate. At times the degree of 'allowance' has occasionally been stretched to breaking point, but what remains is the central, and crucial, organizing principle that gender difference is an essential part of any discussion of the social or symbolic world. Thus between those within and outside feminism is the fundamental division that those within feminism see the world – at least in part – in terms of gender divisions, whilst those outside feminism either refuse or reject the impact of gender difference on individual lives.

It was that assertion of difference, of the radically different experiences of the world of women and men which gave contemporary Western feminism its first great rallying-cry in the late 1960s. The great past of Western feminism – the tradition of Mary Wollstonecraft, Simone de Beauvoir and many others – was known, but only slowly re-discovered.[7] What was said, by Germaine Greer, Kate Millett, Sheila Rowbotham and Shulamith Firestone (and again – and as ever in the history of feminism – many others), was that contemporary sexual politics denigrated and degraded women, and that this denigration took many forms.[8] Reading and reviewing this literature some twenty-five years after its publication still reveals the vitality of the work: at the same time what is now striking about it all is its concern with the West, and its narrowly defined and constructed set of social assumptions. A major target for many of the writers (and this

was true in particular of Greer and Millett) was Western culture
– in all its forms. A major focus was 'high' culture, but feminists
were equally vociferous in attacks on denigratory aspects of
'popular' culture such as the Miss World contest. *Sexual Politics*,
Kate Millett's account of the misogyny of a group of Western
writers is definitively about the inadequacies of Western literature. Similarly, Germaine Greer's *The Female Eunuch*, whilst
being in part a critique of misogyny was also deeply in debt to
high bourgeois culture. Whilst Greer was for more heterosexual
sexuality (at that point in her career) Millett was advocating a
more cautious attitude to heterosexuality, an attitude that was
eventually to emerge as explicit lesbianism.[9]

These works of non-fiction (and Greer and Millett in particular
had close formal links to the academy) were matched by a flow-
ering of feminist fiction.[10] In part, some of this fiction was a re-
discovery of the possibilities of the female bawd, and bawdiness.
(Erica Jong, for example, belongs to this tradition and her *Fear of
Flying* epitomised what was seen as female sexual liberation.) But
the factor that united the fiction and the non-fiction was, more
often than not, a furious plea for women's autonomy, and particularly their sexual autonomy. The sexual revolution was found to
be, as far as women were concerned, deeply inadequate since the
form of sexuality that it prioritized was both heterosexuality and
a form of heterosexuality that took for granted male sexual
desire for women. The rejection of this organizing perception
became a key element of early 1970s feminism: in part the rejection was about the rejection of heterosexuality *per se* (and the
United States in particular saw the emergence of a powerful and
vital lesbian literature of which Jill Johnston – the author of
Lesbian Nation – was perhaps the best known writer) but it was
also about the more complex rejection of a particular form of
heterosexuality in which women 'succumbed' to 'natural' male
desire. As was soon pointed out by gay men, this set of assumptions trapped men, quite as much as women, within a straight-
jacket of expectations about sexual behaviour. Thus the frantic
heterosexuality of the late 1960s was rapidly taken to task by
both women and men for the limits, rather than the extended
possibilities, that it imposed on human actions.

In the cluster of best-selling feminist works of the early 1970s there is a rich vein of fury at misogyny and a general determination to persuade women to self-realization. Two key slogans that emerged from this time and this literature were 'the personal is the political' and 'sisterhood is powerful'. (The latter was also the title of a collection of essays by Robin Morgan.)[11] Both slogans implicitly endorsed the idea that women were universally oppressed and exploited, and that only through a recognition of this common situation could women change the structures that oppressed them. An argument of Engels, that in marriage women are the proletariat and men the bourgeoisie, was one that had much currency, even outside circles sympathetic to Marxism.[12] For some feminists, any participation in a heterosexual relationship carried with it inevitable exploitation; this was a situation, it was asserted, in which negotiation was neither possible nor desirable. From this theoretical position, in which the major organizing dynamic of human history was men's hostility to women, it was inevitable that its adherents would interpret all history and all social relations in terms of war between the sexes. 'Women Only' bookshops, cafés and living space became the practical results of this interpretation of the world, and within it differences between women became vastly less important than the common cause of women against men.

This theoretical position, to which the label 'radical lesbian' or 'radical feminist' is sometimes attached is associated with the writings of women such as Sheila Jeffreys and Mary Daly.[13] It is a position of engaging coherence, in that social divisions become very simple, indeed positively singular and can be identified in terms of gender divisions. At the same time, this very theoretical position also became the point at which other feminists began to offer interpretations of the social position of women that called into question solidarity and – most important – similarity between women, and offered instead ideas about difference and *lack* of common cause. The crucial arguments here were about race and class; in the early 1970s, Marxists offered readings of Marx and Engels that subsumed the sex war to the class war; the times were changing, but not changing enough for the great theoretical systems of the modern world to give way easily to ideas that seemed to complicate, rather than illuminate.

11

This reference – to the 'great theoretical systems of the modern world' – is the point at which the emergence of contemporary feminism has to be situated not just in terms of a changing culture in the West, but in terms of a shift in our theoretical understanding of the world. Thus two major changes have to be noted if we are to situate feminism accurately. The first is the globalization of the late-twentieth-century world, the second is the shift from modernity to post-modernity. The first involves us in re-thinking our perceptions of nationality and ethnicity; we still have national identities, but the meaning of these identities becomes increasingly negotiable (as the post-1989 world demonstrates) and increasingly unstable as global markets, and a global economy unite countries and cultures in ever closer ties. The nature of these ties is frequently exploitative, 'the North' (as prosperous industrialized countries are termed) takes unremittingly from 'the South' in a way that has changed little from the days of blatant nineteenth-century imperialism. Thus to think about women in terms of race now involves far more than thinking about racial divisions within societies; it involves thinking about racial divisions and distinctions between societies quite as much as within national boundaries. To assume, for example, that 'women of colour' necessarily constitute a political group distinct from white women would now be thought an over-simplification. We recognize that the differences between, say, women of Palestine and women of Israel might be considerable in political terms but limited in terms of the material difference between both groups of women and women in, for example, the Sudan. Who is united with whom, and for what reason, has come to be acknowledged as an almost impossibly complex question.

What the above seems to imply is that feminism has now reached such a point of fragmentation that few of the old certainties about sisterhood and unity have any meaning. In one sense this is true, and the movement slogans of the early 1970s ('sisterhood is powerful' for example) now have a dated and a problematic ring to them. Nevertheless, around certain issues (abortion is one of the most obvious instances) women continue to organize across class and racial lines. Equally, just as feminist theorists have begun to be sceptical about the usefulness of the category of 'woman', so international agencies have initiated debates and programmes that call for the empowerment and the education of women.[14] In these programmes (such as that launched in 1994 in Cairo on Family Planning by the United Nations) the term 'women' was used with an inclusiveness that has long disappeared from general use in Western feminist circles.

The exception to this shift is, of course, the 'women' in Women's Studies. In this context, women remain a clear and obvious category, an explicit assertion that in the academic context at least there are similarities and common causes that tie women together. In the past ten years attempts have been made to contest the term 'Women's Studies', and to substitute for it the term 'Gender Studies'. Considerable controversy has been generated by the suggestion that Women's Studies somehow speaks to the past, in which gender differences were not recognized. Further, it is asserted that the term 'gender' rather than 'women' alerts students and teachers alike to the complexity of issues relating to relations between the sexes. Women, it is pointed out, do not live or act in a world from which men are absent; what it is therefore essential to study, this argument continues, is the dynamic of relations between the sexes.[15]

There is considerable appeal in this argument in that at first sight it seems to offer a way out of the impasse of studies that concentrate exclusively on women, without reference to a larger context, or to one peopled by men as well as women.[16] Yet at the same time, what we can set against this appeal are two salient factors: first, that the very term 'Women's Studies' is a constant, and constantly politicizing, reminder that women have been, until relatively recently, largely excluded from the academic curriculum both as subjects and as agents. Until the 1970s it is possible to say that on the whole (and there were of course important exceptions) Western universities taught little that was explicitly about women. In a sense, it also has to be said that the same universities taught little that was explicitly about men. The problem was that the human subject (as the anthropology text book which begins with the sentence 'People in all societies have wives' attested) was simply assumed to be male. The most often cited example of the academic implications of this idea was that of the question of work. In 1970 it was taken-for-granted that work meant paid work, generally performed by men, outside the home. The idea – and the assumptions behind it – was spectacularly shattered by numerous feminist writers, who pointed out that work was very often unpaid, equally often performed by women and absolutely socially essential.[17] The British writer Ann Oakley was amongst those who demonstrated the contribution women made to any economy in their unpaid work.[18] On the other side of the Channel, Christine Delphy demonstrated that the contribution of women to family businesses was as essential as it was generally unrewarded.[19] In the case of France, Delphy's work led to the recognition of women's work by the French government; in Britain, the award of allowances to 'carers' has its origins in the passionate vigour of feminist writing in the early 1970s about work.

Hence 'work on work' provided for feminists a very real instance of the way in which it is crucial to identify women *per se* in debates and discussions, since without this identification, it is all too easy for women to disappear and for the human actor to be assumed to be uniformly male. Making explicit the unpaid work done by women in the home (and indeed in other contexts as well) made it possible to open up discussions about caring, about development policies that ignored or marginalized women, about emotional as well as material work and, indeed, the history of work itself.[20] In this latter context, the extension of ideas about work made possible the re-thinking of ideas about the public and the private and the nature of citizenship. But in the early 1970s many of these developments were in the future; the debates at the time took the form of argument about the contribution of women's unpaid work to the accumulation of surplus labour, the documentation of women's work and their part in the construction of industrial society and radical interventions about the social construction of skill (and with that, of course, the reward system of the West).[21]

It is, as always, difficult (and dangerous) to single out names of individuals who contributed to these debates. The meetings of feminists that took place throughout the West (for example, the Conference at Ruskin College in 1971) were attended by hundreds of women whose names never appeared in print, but who nevertheless made significant contributions to the debates, not least through the sense of urgency and solidarity that their presence created. 'Being there' was a major part played by a whole generation of women. Yet whilst making this claim for the place in history of those who created a sustained enthusiasm, there emerged from that generation many women who were to make a singular and lasting contribution to debates about gender and the lived experience of women. It is difficult to single out individuals, but those who made distinctive contributions *included* (on the British side of the Atlantic) Sheila Rowbotham, Sheila Jeffreys, Veronica Beechey and Juliet Mitchell. In the United States, Kate Millett, Shulamith Firestone, Adrienne Rich and Audré Lorde made interventions of great power and originality, as did, in France, Hélène Cixous and Luce Irigaray.[22] As justification for this list, rather than another, I would offer the explanation that what these women did was to develop in certain crucial ways the feminist tradition. For example, two of the best known feminists of the 1970s in the West were Betty Friedan and Germaine Greer. In *The Feminine Mystique* (first published in 1963) and *The Female Eunuch* (first published in 1970) Betty Friedan and Germaine Greer wrote texts that captured the public imagination and inspired considerable comment. Yet Friedan and Greer's books (as Maggie Humm's exemplary *Feminisms* makes clear) can be placed firmly within existing traditions in feminism: Betty Friedan's account of the malaise of white, middle-class, educated women living in the suburbs of the United States is a plea for more women to receive more education that fits exactly into a long tradition of liberal Western feminism.[23] To read Mary Wollstonecraft's *A Vindication of the Rights of Woman* at the same time as Friedan demonstrates that the singularity and similarity of the Enlightenment vision could easily span differences of continents and a hundred-and-fifty years. Equally, Germaine Greer's account, in *The Female Eunuch*, of the emasculation of women by patriarchy is fuelled by the same energy as the women writers of the seventeenth and eighteenth century who protested at the sexual limitations placed upon them. The right to sexual desire by women had been an issue long before Greer.

15

Thus some of the writing which appeared in the early 1970s spoke as much to earlier traditions as to emerging ones. That there was a feminist tradition in the West – and has been since well before the Enlightenment – has always been known, and feminists of the 1970s were not the first to point out that for centuries women had campaigned for autonomy and for those social rights restricted to men. Campaigning organizations such as, in Britain, the Fawcett Society had long histories of intervention in social and public policy. However, what distinguishes the writers listed above (Rowbotham et al.) from others is that they seized on two ideas which are profoundly radical in their implications and have enormous significance for anyone interested in the question of the construction of knowledge. The first issue that these women identified is that sexual difference has far more profound effects on human thought than has so far been imagined: it was not, therefore, a question about what men thought, but how men thought. The second issue identified at this time was the assertion that differences of gender manifested themselves in all aspects of behaviour.

In the early 1970s many of the ills of the West, and its intellectual assumptions, were grouped together under the term 'Patriarchy'. This idea – and the relevance of the idea – was hotly debated at the time, but even amongst those who were most suspicious about its applicability there was a general acceptance of the idea that in all societies and in all cultures men dominated the public world and through this domination controlled and defined the behaviour of women.[24] Thus 'patriarchal' systems of law made assumptions about the sexual behaviour of women and through these assumptions legally enforced definitions of 'good' and 'bad' women. The most obvious example of patriarchy at work in law in the West was the practice in rape cases of introducing information about the sexual history and appearance of women who had been raped. Women with considerable numbers of sexual relationships or a manner of dress and demeanour that was deemed to be 'suggestive' were subjected to vicious character assassinations at the hands of defence lawyers, operating within an *acceptable* framework of sexual values.[25] The point was, therefore, not that the law or the legal system was invoking an

16

extraordinary set of principles in its defence of accused rapists, but that there existed a set of assumptions about women's appropriate sexual behaviour that could be used to the disadvantage of individual women. In part these assumptions were drawn from the age-old distinction (particularly marked in the West) between virgins and whores. The distinction (sometimes also expressed as Madonnas and Magdalenes or good girls and bad girls) has become widely used (and equally widely criticized) in the West. In the early 1970s it was, however, a relatively novel ingredient in discussions about ideologies about women; and as such it contributed to the construction of a case against the collection of ideas about women known as 'patriarchy'.

But 'the trouble with patriarchy' as a famous article pointed out, was that it tended to obscure individual differences (between individual women and individual circumstances) in favour of an all-embracing theory of sexual relations in which a universal system of patriarchy, and patriarchal knowledge, oppressed all women.[26] This idea had enormous possibilities for political mobilization, in that women could recognize that their individual difficulties were related to general patterns, but at the same time the problem was that women were left in an – apparently – powerless situation, and one in which differences between women were obscured. Differences of class and colour in particular were rapidly shown to be as significant for women as for men, and with this assertion some of the confidence of the concept of patriarchy began to disappear. But the idea has played – and in some senses continues to play – an enormously important part in suggesting that relations between the sexes involve questions of power, both social and political. The power of patriarchy to control all individual behaviour of all individual women may, therefore, be highly differentiated, but the point is that all women are potentially vulnerable to a system of thought that is not always evident.

Thus what emerged in the early 1970s within feminism was a sense of enormous urgency about the need to re-define and re-interpret the social world. A major *locus* of that project rapidly became the academy, in the most general sense of both the universities as institutions and the intellectual networks associated

17

with them. Many of the significant feminist writers of the 1970s
were, in fact, either full-time academics (or ex-academics as was
the case for Greer and Millett) or closely associated with other
liberal professions. As an identifiable feminist presence and
protest emerged, so organized feminist networks began to multi-
ply. (By the end of the 1970s there were networks of women in
publishing, women in law and so on.) All these networks produced and absorbed feminist writing and thus provided a significant readership and authorship for the detailed discussion of
feminist issues that was to emerge by the end of the 1970s. The
pattern of engagement would generally be as follows: a book
would be written and published about women and a particular
subject (for example, Elizabeth Wilson on *Women and the
Welfare State*) and then the implications of the general thesis of
that book would be worked out in specific related contexts. It
was not so much that only a few figures recognized the general
theses, but that the recognition by a generation of women of significant issues encouraged the writing of widely-read texts, which
then led to further debate.

In Britain, the United States and France, the 1970s therefore
saw the rapid growth of publishing by women for women.
Journals and magazines, information networks and professional
associations were established to provide the infrastructural support and development for feminism, and feminist intervention in
the academy. The rapidity of this process was, in retrospect,
striking. What had been, in 1970, a handful of books by women,
had become, by 1980, a library-full of non-fiction and fiction by
and for women. (Some of the material, it has to be said, was part
of a re-claimed past: the example of the Virago Classics series is
precisely such an instance of the re-organization and re-catego-
rization of history that feminism created.) But with this growth in
the literature of feminism came the awareness of two complex
issues. The first was that of the problem of feminism's relation to
the academy, and with it a concern for 'theory' rather than 'reality'. The second was that of the domination of feminism by
white, heterosexual, Western women. *Feminist Review* (one of
the most significant feminist journals established in the 1970s)
published an article in its sixth issue by Eva Kaluzynska entitled

'Wiping the Floor with Theory', a title that caught precisely many of the feelings of growing unease about the intellectualization of feminism. As the cartoons, and the text, of the article point out, a sophisticated understanding and engagement with the theoretical issues relating to the status of housework is often a considerable distance from its practice. Moreover, the *making* of the theory about housework (or about any other area of women's lives) is often not done by the women most centrally involved. Thus what feminism did was to develop a critique of the 'expert' that was not new in Western culture, but was a very specific and detailed response to what was assumed to be a take-over of women's experiences by the habits and practices that had originated in a male academy. A central argument of feminist research in the late 1970s and 1980s was therefore to be the discussion of the place of the subject in research.

In this concern for the safe-guarding of the integrity of individual experience, feminism followed, to a certain extent, a road already established by critics of Western social research. C.W. Mills, best known for his studies of Western elites wrote, in a review of *The Second Sex* published in 1953 that:

> She has written one of those books that remind us how little we really *think* about our own personal lives and problems, and she invites us and helps us to do so.[27]

That suggestion was hardly taken up in the West in the two decades that followed. The social sciences, and indeed the humanities, dominated as they were by men, were centrally concerned with the description and the analysis of the public world. The famous British community studies of the period (the closest literature that there was at the time to the delineation of 'real' life) by Michael Young, Peter Willmott and others was about 'private' life seen by active participants in the public world.[28] Equally, critical voices amongst left-wing male academics (for example Talal Asad on anthropology) pointed out, as was to be echoed later by feminist writers, that many academics assumed an unthinking attitude of power and dominance towards their subjects.[29] Asad's collection of essays entitled *Anthropology and the Colonial Encounter* defined a critique that is pertinent to this day.

It is, therefore, around the issues of power and control that feminism developed its own critique of the academy. But, and it is a crucially significant but, at the same time as white, Western feminists within (or close to) the academy were developing their critique of patriarchal knowledge, other women were raising difficult issues about the difference in power not just between women and men but between women and women. Dissent around that issue was visible from the earliest days of contemporary feminism, but differences of opinion became strikingly evident by the late 1970s and early 1980s. In 1982 Hazel Carby published an article entitled 'White woman listen! Black feminism and the boundaries of sisterhood', that effectively attacked the idea that sisterhood was in racial terms, an unproblematic term. Hazel Carby wrote:

> it is very important that white women in the women's movement examine the ways in which racism excludes many black women and prevents them from unconditionally aligning themselves with white women. . . . Black women do not want to be grafted into 'feminism' in a tokenistic manner as colourful diversions to 'real' problems. Feminism has to be transformed if it is to address us. Neither do we wish our words to be misused in generalities as if what each one of us utters represents the total experience of all black women.[30]

Hazel Carby's critique was taken up by other non-white women, and contributed to a growing sense amongst feminists, and feminist academics, that what had once been a movement that could potentially embrace all women had become a fragmented and often divided consciousness. The language of feminism thus began to change and the terms 'oppression', 'subordination' and 'exploitation' that had been widely used and widely integrated into much-used texts became increasingly rare, as women recognized the difficulties, and pitfalls, in using these terms. And as feminism's vocabulary changed, so did that of the social sciences and humanities in general: post-modernity offered a widely endorsed critique of the great synthesizing theories of the nineteenth century and proposed instead (à la Foucault) that the way to interpret life in the late twentieth century was through participation within, and engagement with, a series of over-lapping discourses and identities.[31] This approach to the social, and emotional world, made perfect sense to many feminists in that it allowed differences in gender and sexual identity, and gave theoretical space to the multi-faceted lives of women. Those social theories – of which Marxism is the best example – that had prioritized participation in the public world of paid labour had inevitably marginalized women since their role in that world was often limited. Furthermore, the social theories based in the examination of the 'public' had provided no space for the discussion of the 'private' world, emotional life, and sexuality. In all, subjective experience was largely absent from Marxist and structuralist accounts of social life.

The impetus to develop, and to endorse, theoretical systems that allowed the subjective, came largely from the centrality that feminism gave to the understanding of sexuality. The sexual politics of the 1970s brought two issues to the forefront of the political agenda: a critique of the dominance of heterosexuality (which was informed by both lesbian and gay literature and experience) and an equally powerfully-charged critique of the power relations of heterosexuality. The latter issue was fuelled by the de-privatization (to borrow a term) of domestic violence, sexually abusive relationships within the household, the institutional management (or mis-management) of sexuality and the visual and literary representation of heterosexuality. Both these critiques have led to the development of rich academic and critical literatures.[32] Lesbian and gay studies have re-discovered a past and presented an account of the history of sexuality in which the diversity of sexual practice is an evident and central theme.[33] Equally, feminist cultural studies have shown how the representation of women is replete with questions about the relative power of the sexes; sexual negotiation and contest has thus been demonstrated as a central theme of Western culture.

But little of this work, in whatever academic area or whatever context of the social and institutional world, would have been possible without the vitalizing impact of the politics of the women's movement. For many women, the women's movement provided a sense of unity and shared experience that created the

confidence and the sense of certainty essential for the development of radical ideas. Equally, those ideas would probably have
developed less of their theoretical complexity and intellectual
energy without the input of psycho-analytic theory to feminism
from the mid-1970s onwards. Juliet Mitchell's *Psychoanalysis
and Feminism* re-opened the pages of Freud for feminism and in
so doing allowed access to an understanding of the symbolic and
the emotional world. There was, and is, plenty of material in
Freud that remains unacceptable for many feminists, but at the
same time his theory of the unconscious and of acquired sexual
identity allow access to the discussion of the metaphorical in the
social world and the dynamic of the processes through which
sexual identity is acquired. Crucially, psycho-analysis seemed to
offer a way out of the static analysis of sex roles offered by
Anglo-American social science. From the re-reading of Freud
came, therefore, the discussion of women as 'sign' and the reading of literature in terms of general patterns rather than individual experiences.[34] Moreover, with interest in Freud's ideas came a
related interest in the works of other, and largely continental,
psycho-analytically informed writers. Lacan and Kristeva were
just two of the theorists who became widely influential, if not
widely read.[35]

It is thus that we can now look back on almost twenty-five
years of feminist writing and speak confidently of the establishment of feminist theory, and with it the academic area known as
Women's Studies. Tensions still exist around the very presence of
feminism-in-the-academy, in that the academy is (if not to the
women in it) a privileged place, and a place in which Western
dominance is absolute. For many women, feminist academics are
part of an elite, divorced from the practices and problems of the
'real' world. These tensions – and occasional hostilities – are nevertheless tempered by an acceptance of the recognition of diverse
'sites of struggle', in which individuals in any institution have to
contest particular rather than general issues. Equally, the confidence with which we can speak of the establishment of feminism
in the academy and feminist theory is qualified by the massive
empirical under-representation of women as academics, and the
limited access that women still have to institutional knowledge.

Thus what follows in the subsequent chapters is an account of an extraordinarily rich intellectual development – but rich in intellectual vitality rather than institutional support.

2
Public and Private: Women and the State

One of the most radical ideas of contemporary feminism is its contention that the 'private' space of the household and the family should be subject to public scrutiny. The idea is complex, and complicated, because as well as asking awkward questions about the sexual division of power in the household, it calls into question many liberties and freedoms that have taken centuries to construct. For many women – subject to male violence in the home or the prisoners of traditional patriarchal expectations about women-as-carers – tearing away the cover of secrecy around the home offers liberation, if only in the recognition that their position is shared by other women as well.[1] But for other women, the increased licence of public scrutiny into private life brings with it only intrusion and, in the worst cases, unwanted interference. The spectre of the state, in its full Janus-like reality of protector and oppressor, becomes the crucial issue and has become so for feminist academics for a variety of reasons, not the least of which is the possibility of constructing, through the academy, the necessary arguments to shift specific state policies. Thus, for women, the state has been both oppressive (in its masculinist ideology) and liberatory (in the opportunities it offers for mitigation of control by individual men).

It is this relationship, of women to the state, that provides the *locus* around which we can organize feminist literature on the public and the private. In the industrial West, the traditional relationship of women to the state has been distant. For centuries, indeed well into the nineteenth century, women had little or nothing to do with state power. Obviously, female monarchs, and those influential British aristocratic women re-discovered by Linda Colley, exercised either direct power (in the case of the former) or influence (in the case of the latter).[2] But women *per se* were excluded from the church, the law and politics, the three essential structures of public power. In this, it has to be said that women shared the same status (or lack of it) with the majority of men, since in most European countries political and social power was held, until well into the nineteenth century, by a small group of men. In Britain, for example, male suffrage was limited until the late nineteenth century, and every subsequent study of every elite has confirmed the inter-generational replication of social power.[3] Thus in considering women and power – and women and public life – the first caution that is necessary concerns the assumption that all men had an equal access to public power that was absent for all women. Society was, and is, stratified along class lines, and large numbers of the male population have always been effectively excluded from any effective exercise of public power.

But even with this note of caution about the empirical reality of men's relationship to public power, it is still possible to argue that the general assumption made by men about the public world is that it is a male domain.[4] The original construction of the Enlightenment understanding of the term 'citizen' was organized around male experience – an experience that included personal autonomy and mobility, independence of choice and access to (and involvement in) the articulation of symbolic and scientific knowledge. When Jane Austen's heroine Anne Elliot spoke of women's experience of the world in *Persuasion* she encapsulated the nature of this difference:

> Men have had every advantage of us in telling their own story. Education has been theirs in so much higher a degree; the pen has been in their hands.[5]

Nor was Austen alone in pointing out this difference: some twenty-six years before the publication of *Persuasion* Mary Wollstonecraft had identified, in *A Vindication of the Rights of Woman*, the assumptions that underpinned the exclusion of women from the public world; those assumptions were, she argued, typified in particular by Rousseau who glorified the idea of a lonely-man-in-nature and largely marginalized social ties. Thus she wrote:

> Public education, of every denomination, should be directed to form citizens; but if you wish to make good citizens, you must first exercise the affections of a son and a brother. This is the only way to expand the heart; for public affections, as well as public virtues, must ever grow out of the private character.[6]

Indeed what she proposes is the theme of much of the dialogue between women and men throughout the nineteenth and twentieth centuries – the negotiation by women for more presence in the public world and, crucially, the equally significant demand that men have to be judged in private as well as public terms.

The recognition by Mary Wollstonecraft in 1792 of the issue of the public and the private is a crucial point in the history of women, men and the state. Wollstonecraft saw that men could easily become party to a view of themselves that only recognized public achievement; equally, she allowed that excluding women from 'civil existence' led to the domination of the trivial:

> Females, in fact, denied all political privileges, and not allowed, as married women, excepting in criminal cases, a civil existence, have their attention naturally drawn from the interest of the whole community to that of the minute parts, though the private duty of any member of society must be very imperfectly performed when not connected with the general good. The mighty business of female life is to please, and restrained from entering into more important concerns by political and civil oppression, *sentiments become events*. (my emphasis)[7]

This last idea might have been read by Jane Austen, for no author has ever captured so clearly the results of domestic seclusion as Austen did in Mrs Bennet in *Pride and Prejudice*. Indeed, the Bennets illustrate particularly clearly the public and private split which Wollstonecraft is attacking: Mr Bennet, the educated and intelligent hero of the Enlightenment is in point of fact a careless and metaphorically 'absent' father. Left to shoulder the cares of the household, and the future of her children, Mrs Bennet becomes a figure traditionally interpreted as ridiculous and comic. Yet how else, we can rhetorically ask, was the poor woman supposed to act, faced with the prospect of penury for herself and her daughters, should Mr Bennet die prematurely.

It was, of course, to safeguard the Mrs Bennets of the world that the state began to take on those responsibilities that individual Mr Bennets chose to ignore or reject. The situation of widows, of fatherless children, brought into being the hideous Victorian system of workhouses, but subsequently the more compassionate, if hardly more lavish, provision of state pensions and child benefits. The tortuous route to this provision is one in which the interests of women and men were often contradictory and equally frequently contested. Barbara Taylor, in *Eve and the New Jerusalem*, has vividly told the story of the struggle by working-class women for the recognition of their work and its proper economic reward. The title of one of that author's articles on the issue ('The Men are as Bad as their Masters') tells us much about the coincidence and similarity of the assumptive worlds of both working-class and bourgeois men. Disunited by class, they were united in gender politics, in that they saw the place of women in the home and not in the workplace. In a further example, on a similar theme, Jane Humphries has discussed the attitude of women and men to protective legislation in the early nineteenth century: for men, the struggle was less to facilitate the conditions of women's paid labour than to exclude them from it.[8] In the appalling and debilitating situations of early nineteenth-century factories and mines was established the idea of the 'Family Wage': a wage sufficient for men to support their wives and families and the subject of critical feminist scrutiny in the late twentieth century.[9] Thus male responsibility for the family was accomplished with the consequence of female economic dependence. Mrs Bennet, to return to *Pride and Prejudice*, recognized that without husbands her daughters could starve.

But of course many women, without male economic support,

27

did not starve, and they did not starve because they worked – either as servants, or in factories or in the other options available to them in the nineteenth century. Yet at the same time as they were doing this (and whether married or not were taking whatever work was available) they were doing so within the framework of an ideology that essentially saw the role of women as wives and mothers. Throughout the nineteenth and twentieth century, British (and North American and Northern European) history is replete with examples of struggles by women to re-negotiate this relationship, at the same time as they were also attempting to 'domesticate' men and question expectations about the 'double standard' of sexual morality.[10] The re-negotiation was clearly often personal – in that individual women often questioned male assumptions about the proper role of women – but it was also increasingly organized, and by the end of the nineteenth century every major industrial society had seen the emergence of campaigns for women's education, entry to the professions, legal emancipation and right to vote. The campaigns were fought and won in different ways (and at different times) in different countries, but all were about citizenship, and the degree to which women could participate in the public world. Yet often institutional barriers fell before attitudes changed: for example, women were admitted to the medical profession long before (very long before) medicine's view of the female body was re-interpreted in anything like a female understanding. The case of the relationship of women to the law is analogous: women were allowed to practise as lawyers very long before the assumptions of the law about women were subject to any kind of feminist criticism.

Thus, in the history of the relationship of women to the state, it is necessary to take a cautious view of an emancipatory model. Women, and particularly middle-class women, were able to benefit from some of the changes that occurred in gendered gate-keeping. All women benefited from the gradual development of a welfare state; improvements in medicine and child health gave support to all mothers and diminished the endless grief endured by mothers in the nineteenth century who very often watched their children die. It would be foolish to suppose that the state

28

acted from universally 'pure' motives of altruism: as Anna Davin has pointed out, the British State began its ponderous progress towards state responsibility for children because of revelations about the physical health (or lack of it) of men as potential soldiers.[11] (Hence the Boer War fits into the historians model of war as an engine for social change and social improvement.)[12] Nor was it ever the case that those making policies for state intervention in health and welfare left behind their assumptions about class and gender: the history of Fabian socialism, for example, is full of examples in which the term 'mothers' has to be read as a coded reference to working-class women. Indeed, this code reached its full maturity in the 1944 Beveridge Report, in which the British post-war Welfare State was designed with very clear gender stereotypes in mind: men supported their wives and families, and only single women were to be regarded as autonomous individuals.[13]

The view of women contained in Beveridge represented what we can see as a twentieth-century codification of women: a codification that essentially limited the social and symbolic options of women. For women in the nineteenth (and indeed the eighteenth) century, all the evidence suggests that, whatever the nature of formal social and legal codes, there was considerable scope for independent and unconventional action by women. The codes were there, but the ability of society to enforce them was limited. But the development of state bureaucracies, the society of 'discipline and punishment' as Foucault describes it, brought with it a limitation, as well as an improvement, in the situation of women. Thus at the same time as the state extended a degree of assistance to women, so it demanded acquiescence in its expectations about women. Increasingly, an ancient Western distinction between 'Madonnas and Whores' began to have an institutional meaning as state provision and state regulation demanded a human meaning for its structures. Hence by 1944 – and the publication in Britain of the Beveridge Report – the state had developed an understanding of the 'good' women whom it saw itself as deemed to protect, and the 'bad' women who were outside its protective jurisdiction. The relationship was summed up in 1978 by Mary McIntosh in a key paper:

29

One of the features of capitalist societies, especially in the more advanced stages of capitalism, is the important part played by the state in the economy and in the society at large. It is not surprising, therefore to find that the state plays a part in the oppression of women. In this paper it will be argued that the state does this not directly but through its support for a specific form of household: the family household dependent largely upon a male wage and upon female domestic servicing.[14]

This *ideal* of the family was, of course, one that bore little or no relationship to many actual families, or real social relationships. What it did was to marginalize other forms of households: those headed by women, those formed by gay or lesbian partners and, most strikingly in the late 1980s as recession took hold, households in which men did not have jobs and thus no 'male wage' with which to support their families. This removal of the basic assumption of Beveridge – that men would have jobs – has had the now well-established effect of creating a generation of men who have never had (or will never have again) paid employment and women who have no expectation of financial support by men. The feminist slogans in the 1970s about resisting economic dependence by women on men have taken on a bitter and ironical twist, since for many women, and their children, such dependence has never been available. Increasing numbers of women, often demonized as 'single mothers' have had to turn to the state for basic economic support, as the likelihood of support by male partners has disappeared.

What high rates of male unemployment in Britain have done to relations between the sexes (and to a generation of children) remains a matter of contention; Beatrix Campbell, for example, has written persuasively of the social and personal pressures produced by male unemployment.[15] The Right has created moral panics about 'unmarried mothers', and women who 'marry' the state, whilst the Centre and the Left (both feminist and otherwise) have pointed out that women and children have to depend on the state, in the absence of secure male employment and that for many women dependence on state benefit, however limited, is infinitely preferable to dependence on an individual man who may equate economic provision with personal domination. Thus on this issue – of changing patterns of family and economic life – there develops a cluster of problems relating to women and the state. First, the obvious breakdown of the condition of full male employment on which female economic dependence could depend. Second, the increasing refusal of women to accept the unspoken contract of the Beveridge family – that in return for economic support they would provide unpaid domestic services for their husbands and families and – at the same time – tolerate patriarchal authority in the home. Third, the changing nature of capitalism throughout Europe from the end of the Second World War transformed people as producers of goods into consumers of goods: to participate in the new culture of consumption, individuals (male or female) needed money, and access to money became ideologically – as well as materially – crucial. Women, but most particularly mothers, found that their participation in this new culture was effectively blocked by lack of independent financial resources. The absence of childcare, the low level of educational and professional achievement of many women and the refusal of male partners to re-negotiate the domestic contract created a growing sense of dissatisfaction with the existing construction of family life.

This transformation of Western culture since 1945 has therefore revolutionized expectations, male and female, about social and sexual relationships. The cultural shift in the West to what Barbara Ehrenreich described as 'recreational sex', together with the change in codes about pre-marital chastity and the disappearance of the stigma about divorce and co-habitation has effectively changed the pattern of the lives of millions of Western people.[16] Yet at the same time as this has occurred, what has not changed is the economic impact of the birth of children on women, and the continuing assumption that the responsibility of caring for others (whether young or old) lies with women. It is now the case that half the British work force is female, but what that means in greater detail is that most women (the majority of whom are mothers) work in low paid, insecure, part-time jobs. 'Good' jobs, in the sense of jobs which are full-time, backed by long-term benefits and expectations of life-long employment, remain largely the preserve of men. To shift this pattern the state would have to

31

intervene on a massive scale to establish comprehensive childcare and to re-write the terms and conditions of employment for part-time workers.

But for ideological reasons, the British State has refused to move in this direction, and this pattern (of leaving women largely responsible for care whatever its impact on their potential or actual employment) is replicated in many industrial societies. It is, moreover, the pattern that has emerged in post-1989 Eastern Europe, in countries (such as East Germany) that previously had a relatively generous provision of childcare.[17] There was, overall, a dramatic contrast between East and West in terms of what the state was expected to provide. The Eastern model, which emphasized the provision of welfare facilities of all kinds, also emphasized and expected that all citizens, male or female, childless or not, would be in employment. The Soviet citizen, or the East German citizen, was therefore more androgynous than the Western equivalent. The problem with this model, as feminists pointed out long before 1989, was that however theoretically blind to gender difference the state might have been individual men were not, and patriarchy (in domestic life and culture) was more than alive and well. The 'double shift', which Western feminists identified in the literature about paid work in the 1970s, was as much a feature of Eastern as Western societies.

Literature on women and the state in Eastern Europe (of which, post 1989, there is an increasing volume) emphasizes both the extent to which the old Soviet state supported the employment of women and yet maintained other forms of implicit sexism. As numerous feminist writers (such as Maxine Molyneux and Barbara Einhorn) have pointed out, political power, whether East or West, belonged to men, and the social construction of the value of paid work was riddled with sexist assumptions on both sides of the West/East divide.[18] If there were more female doctors in the East, it was because medicine was a low-status profession. Nor, it seemed, did the presence of women in medicine produce woman-friendly medicine or medical services. The provision of contraception and the conditions of childbirth – both aspects of medical services crucial to women – were frequently either limited or brutal. Thus by the mid-1980s (indeed before the fall of the Berlin Wall), the feminist literature on the state had reached something of a consensus: following the thesis of Mary McIntosh (in 1978) it was accepted that the Western state (and to a large extent Eastern Europe) legitimated, however ineffectively, a patriarchal view of women. It was assumed by the state that women were economically dependent on men, were assumed to be 'naturally' better suited for caring for others and either 'good' women (who deserved state protection) or 'bad' women (who had to be punished by the state).

During the 1980s, as suggested above, the reality of women's economic dependence on men (which had always been more secure in fantasy than in fact) increasingly broke down. Male unemployment, inflation and the gradual erosion of state-provided facilities increasingly forced many women throughout Europe, as well as in Britain, into paid work. At the same time, and from the 1970s onwards, what changed at least as dramatically was the acceptance by women of other instances of state intervention. Feminist challenges – to the nature of the provision of welfare, the law's discussion of women and to educational policies – became evident and increasingly effective. Again, what was at issue was the institutional construction of the citizen as male – the lurking 'universal male' in institutional practice – and the Virgins/Whores duality of ideological constructions of women. Both these issues came together in two of the great feminist challenges to the British state in the 1970s and the 1980s: the debate over the 1967 Abortion Act in the 1980s and the challenge, from the beginning of the 1970s, to the form and nature of legal interventions on rape and domestic violence. Although both these campaigns were about British policies and practices, similar campaigns took place throughout Europe and North America.

In the case of the debate over abortion, it has to be said that the issue has become one that has, in many countries other than Britain, a very considerable political significance. In the United States, it has become a rallying-cry for the Right, whilst in contemporary Poland it provides a demonstration of the close links between the Polish state and the Catholic church. As Janet Hadley wrote in 1994:

There is little doubt that the bishops of Poland, who behave more like leaders of a political party than as simple guardians of moral values, have their sights set not only on banning abortion but also divorce, provision of contraception, and other hall-marks of a sec-ular society.[19]

The Polish debate over abortion (and its implications for legisla-tion and practice in other parts of Eastern Europe) demonstrates, as Janet Hadley goes on to point out, the extent to which the state (particularly when it represents a sense of national indepen-dence as it does in Poland) can control the lives of women. Even if, as evidence suggests, a majority of women in Poland describe themselves as Roman Catholic, the extent to which they concur with a law that effectively outlaws abortion (at the same time as making it the only means of contraception) is highly question-able. But it also raises the issue – again increasingly significant since the 1980s – of the relationship of women to the state. When women in Poland, or Iran, identified with particular symbols of opposition to an unpopular regime (Roman Catholicism in Poland, Islam in Iran), what it was difficult for women to do was negotiate the terms of their commitment to that form of opposi-tion. Thus opposition to the Shah in Iran led to support for Khomeini, but with it came increasingly patriarchal policies on women.[20]

It is in this context, of the general issue of women and the state, that we have to see the debates in Britain on abortion (and the new medical technology of human reproduction) and women and the law. The 1967 Abortion Act in Britain was introduced (more or less inevitably) by a male Member of Parliament (David Steel) but with the backing of the Abortion Law Reform Society, run and organized by a woman, Diana Munday. In the debates on this Act, which introduced a social clause into the acceptable reasons for legal abortion, women were generally discussed as people with responsibilities other than carrying children. Thus the debate was, at least in part, organized around the right of women to free will and self-determination, and not as agencies of divine providence or male fertility. Classic liberalism therefore worked, in this case, to the advantage of women; by the mid-1980s, when the Corrie Bill was introduced (but defeated) the ground had shifted away from the rights of the woman to the rights of the foetus – a shift that also became the focus, in the United States, for opposition to the 1973 pro-choice Supreme Court decision in *Roe v. Wade.*

This recent change in the discourse of debates about abortion marked a shift that we can observe in the West (and particularly in Britain) away from arguments about the vulnerability of women, towards arguments based on assumptions about sexual equality. It is a shift in discourse that demands attention, since in feminist literature much has been made of the specific social inequalities of women. The model has been described as the 'women as victim' model, and certainly a tradition within feminism has consistently identified women as the victims of male oppression and male violence. Susan Brownmiller's classic study of rape, *Against our Will*, was very much in this mould: the thesis being that women are universally less powerful than men. The problem with the argument, as other feminists were quick to point out, was that considerable differences in social power existed between women and that women played a considerable part in the construction and negotiation of their own interests. Thus the thesis of woman-as-victim, with its concomitant rider of blame-the-victim, produced widespread criticism.

But in reviewing the feminist literature on the public and the private from the 1970s to the 1990s we can see that the underlying theoretical model of the idea of women-as-victims has largely disappeared, in part because of the recognition of women as *agents* as well as victims, but also because of the recognition of diverse and diffuse power structures and discourses of power within contemporary Western society. In this, feminism has been significantly influenced by the work of Michel Foucault, whose lasting heritage to feminism has been the idea of multiple sites of power and knowledge in society.[21] Essentially, what Foucault did was to take issue with the concept of power as a hierarchical structure, in which power was concentrated at the top of the structure and imposed on those below and replace it with a model of the social world that corresponded rather more to a diagram of the solar system: a world in which power was located in different places and in which intervention was generally, and widely, possible. Foucault's ideas, and both their difficulty and importance for feminism, have now been thoroughly examined, but their importance in the 1970s and the 1980s needs to be emphasized, since they allowed women to de-construct the dominant theoretical model of patriarchy as the absolute oppression of women and replace it with a model in which the forms, degrees and contradictions of patriarchy could be allowed.[22] At the same time, Foucault's idea of 'power without a subject' is problematic for feminism in denying the individual, not to mention the collective, power of men rather than women. Nevertheless, the integration of Foucault's ideas – and those from the Continental Marxism of Louis Althusser – led to the development of a different kind of feminist politics: one which recognized that power was everywhere (and everywhere competed for) and that political struggle was therefore omnipresent.[23]

Thus by the beginning of the 1980s, the view of women and the state suggested by Mary McIntosh was beginning to be revised. Few feminists quarrelled with the idea – discussed by McIntosh – that official state policy enshrined and codified particular ideas about women but negotiation with these views was not ruled out as impossible. It was recognized that even if the state continued to maintain an ideal of male and female behaviour, the practices of the state within named institutional contexts could be challenged. Hence feminist literature on women and the state reflects both this changing politics and the changing theoretical model of the state. In the literature on the law, education, the health and welfare services, the challenges by women to the state (the actual working out of women's 'will-to-power') have been articulated and recorded. Within the literature there are numerous examples of this shift, but areas in particular stand out because they have given rise to a very rich feminist literature: the law, medicine and the welfare services. For example, Linda Gordon on working-class women in the United States and Hilary Graham on women and health in Britain have illustrated the range and the depth of women's resistance to patriarchal expectations.[24]

Writing within feminism on the law has been fired, on both sides of the Atlantic, by women's fury at legal judgements in cases, such as rape and divorce, that involve explicit sexual poli-tics. Before feminist pressure, rape victims in England were named, and defence lawyers were allowed to use evidence about the victim's sexual history in court. Thus, for example, the defence could produce statements about a 'three-times married' or 'provocatively dressed' woman with perfect impunity: it was accepted that women 'invited' rape and that male sexual response was uncontrollable if presented with strong enough stimuli. At work here was a model not just of women and the law but of male and female sexuality: 'good' women did not dress in ways likely to inflame male passion, nor did they act in other ways that suggested sexual availability. As long as 'good' women abided by these rules, they were eligible for state protection. If they did not, then it was essentially their fault if they became the victims of sexual attack. English judges were particularly likely to express this account of sexual politics, and the comments by some emi-nent members of the English judiciary have gone down in femi-nist history as evidence of explicit legal misogyny. A number of women academics mounted a concerted campaign on this con-struction of male and female sexual relations: in Britain Carol Smart and Jennifer Temkin are just two of those who have attacked the underlying assumptions of the legal system.[25]

Yet although the workings of the legal system in every Western society have been subject to feminist scrutiny (and found to exhibit the same model of appropriate female behaviour) it would be wrong to assume that these legal systems have radically changed under feminist pressure. Thus feminist literature on the law makes two points: the documentation of the way in which 'the law' (in all its manifestations from behaviour in court to treatment of young offenders and sentencing policy) behaves towards women and girls, and analysis of the causes of this behaviour. What emerges is a picture of a profession largely dominated by men (certainly so in England in terms of barristers and judges rather than solicitors) and still ruled by the assump-tion that the very process of law should treat individuals equally, even though individuals are manifestly unequal and often treated as such. Hence more complex issues about women and the law have begun to emerge on both sides of the Atlantic about the very relevance to women of a law (or laws) based on expectations about citizens-as-men. Since it is apparent that women do not have identical social experiences to those of men, and are more often than men effectively disempowered by those experiences, some feminists have begun to argue that the whole idea of 'one law', a progressive concept in the early nineteenth century, is now actually a regressive one. For example, as Martha Nussbawm has recently pointed out:

> A feminist theory of justice should certainly question whether the unlimited acquisitiveness of modern capitalist societies has always been good for the family, for the bonds of community or, indeed, for sex equality itself. Two people who believe that more income and wealth is always better than less are likely to have difficulties about the division of labour at home that people less attached to acquisition may not have; and professions that are based on this principle impose well-known burdens on their aspiring young members, making it very difficult for them to be just to their partners.[26]

In raising these issues, what Martha Nussbawm is engaging with are two themes that occur over and over again in feminist literature on institutions. The first is the challenge to the idea that institutions are gender blind: the whole weight of the evidence now produced by feminist academics about the West is that institutions (be they schools, hospitals or the law) differentiate systematically, and often radically, between individuals on the grounds of their gender. In the case of the law, Martha Nussbawm suggests, the relationship is even more complex because the whole idea of law in liberal democratic societies is that citizens are equal in the sight of the law, yet the law treats women and men very differently whilst at the same time refusing to recognize many of the differences between them. In recent years, this issue has come to public attention in England through court cases involving the killing, by women, of violent and abusing male partners. On the one hand the law is apparently quite clear that murder is murder, on the other it is recognized that the law (in all Western societies) allows the defence of provocation (*légitime defense*, as it is described in France). Then, as recent cases in England have made transparently clear, the law enters the area of judgement about 'provocation', and how it is regarded as acceptable, or not acceptable, for men to behave towards women.

Through instances such as these it is possible to demonstrate the subjective values and assumptions that guide the actions of individuals within institutions. That these assumptions are gendered is a theme of work on women and medicine, women and education and women and the Welfare State. In the case of women and medicine, a generation of women writing about medicine have pointed out that the organization of modern medicine was constructed around the exclusion of women as doctors and the male body as a norm of human existence. In the case of the former, a considerable literature – from the early 1970s onwards and in particular the publication of the immensely influential pamphlets by Barbara Ehrenreich and Deirdre English on women healers – has documented the exclusion of women-as-healers from professionalized, 'modern' medicine.[27] Thus whilst the profession of midwifery, and many other skills related to healing the sick, were originally the preserve of women, post-Enlightenment, 'modern science', gradually marginalized this contribution by women, and with it a specific understanding of the female body. As women writers on the history of science such as Londa Schiebinger have pointed out, the view of science which prevailed in the post-Enlightenment period was one in which Nature became identified as unruly, irrational and, above all, as female.[28]

In the new world of nineteenth-century science and rationality the 'feminine' as an abstraction, and women as a reality, were largely marginalized by institutional practice. Men were expected to conform to a stereotype of masculine behaviour, in which affectivity was interpreted as weakness, whilst women were constructed as weak, hysterical and intellectually inferior. The 'soft' feminine and the 'hard' masculine then received institutional recognition and confirmation in particular practices. Nevertheless, as numerous women historians have pointed out, at the same time as women were constructed as weak and hysterical, they were also maintaining large households and performing considerable amounts of physical labour. This 'structural contradiction' (to use Marcel Bloch's terminology) was not over-looked by feminists, who from the middle of the nineteenth century campaigned for the right of women to enter the professions, and in this and other ways challenged the institutional world of the late nineteenth and twentieth centuries.[29] Battles were fought and won throughout the West, with the result that in the majority of Western countries women had gained the formal right, by the end of the Second World War, to enter public life and the professions. (Indeed, the civic and legal emancipation of women was so widely recognized in the West by this time as a mark of 'modern' societies, that the enfranchisement of women was imposed by the United States on Japan as part of the post-Hiroshima peace treaty).

Thus by 1945, formal access to institutional power, and to institutions themselves, was allowed to women everywhere in the West. Indeed, during the Second World War women had actually been encouraged by Allied governments (though not by Hitler's Germany) to take up paid work.[30] However, since this encouragement was limited to the war years, the expectation in the period post-1945 was that women would be what became known as 'home-makers'.[31] Few women, in the academy or elsewhere, challenged this model, although a few notable women published work at this time that was highly critical of the post-1945, Cold War, construction of women. One well known example was Simone de Beauvoir's *The Second Sex* (which was first published in France in 1949), whilst others included Viola Klein's *The Feminine Character: History of an Ideology* (first published in 1946) and (less obviously related to feminism but central to its concerns) Mirra Komarovsky's *Blue Collar Marriage* (first published in 1962). What is striking about all these women is that in various ways they had links with left-wing, or dissenting, social movements, social movements that in one way or another questioned the legitimacy of the state. Thus what we see in this period of feminism is that same questioning of the public world that was to motivate much of the literature in the 1970s.

In this questioning of the public world, we can identify the continuation of the tradition of Mary Wollstonecraft suggested earlier: a tradition that had called into question the idea of universalism, and men as the central human actor. As Margaret

Stacey and Marion Price were to point out in 1981 in *Women, Power and Politics*, women have largely been excluded from public power. In an essay published in 1994 Meg Stacey reflected on the importance of analysing the 'ordinary' world, in order to demonstrate the ways in which the workings of that world constructed the means through which women became, and remained, disempowered.[32] Thus her goal (particularly in the case of work on the General Medical Council) was to demonstrate the ways in which the *apparently normal* (my italics) led to processes of exclusion on the grounds of gender and race. What emerges from this work is a thesis about the failure of an institution (in this case the General Medical Council) to fulfil public expectations of its universal value. As Meg Stacey wrote:

> My aim in writing *Regulating British Medicine* was to expose the pro-professional – and also masculinist and racist - characteristics of the GMC, hoping thereby to encourage practitioners to see what I believed I saw: namely, that although the members were well-meaning, hard-working people (mostly men) who sincerely believed they were doing a good job, in practice they were not adequately fulfilling their statutory function of protecting the public.[33]

The point that emerged from Stacey's work, and that of many other women throughout the West, was that institutions had prejudices, amongst which sexism and racism were particularly noticeable. In the case of other aspects of medicine, and medical institutions, researchers such as Ann Oakley demonstrated the value judgements made by male doctors about women. In *From Here to Maternity* (published in 1981) Oakley documented the ways in which the medicalization of childbirth had come to dominate Western practice, a form of medicine constructed by men about women. Indeed, a considerable literature on women and health has now become a core concern of feminism: the roots lie in the thesis, argued in the 1970s, that male medicine misunderstands the female body, but the debates have now extended to cover all aspects of women's health, other than those of childbirth and reproduction. Obviously, there are differences in the literature between different countries (most strikingly between Britain and the United States where health care is organized and financed in different ways) but even between cultures, there is a general consensus that medicine, like the law, is dominated by male practitioners who act on the premise that the human subject of their endeavours is male. As feminists have pointed out, neither of these assumptions is justifiable: in all Western societies most of the people who work in medicine are female (for example, 95 per cent of the nurses in the UK are women) and women use the health services, if not the law, more than men do.

Thus feminism in the 1970s and 1980s could confidently claim to have demonstrated the disjunction between supposed institutional objectivity and actual institutional prejudice. Medicine and the law have become contested areas, as have education and the welfare services.[34] The arguments in these latter instances are made in the same way as the case of the former: the institution's values are defined as non-gendered, its practice is then demonstrated as deeply gendered. In the instance of education, the concentration of girls in the humanities and the social sciences and the continued espousal of the academy of the concept of universal knowledge have all received considerable attention.[35] Equally (as is certainly the case for medicine) the evidence collected by feminists has led to growing institutional awareness of the deficiencies and sexism of specific institutional practices. For example, greater choice in the management of childbirth is now more available to more women in Britain, just as the identification of 'fear of maths' in girls has led to the development of programmes to counteract it.

Thus in many ways it can be said that the 1970s and the 1980s saw the emergence of an extensive feminist critique of the public, institutional world, which had an impact both on library shelves and the real world. Yet at the same time as this critique emerged (and with it pressure groups organized around issues relating to women's health, education, legal welfare rights), there remained an overwhelming consensus that the agenda of the public world was still set by men, and shaped by discourses that gave a priority to the public world and the imperatives of the capitalist market. Throughout the West in the 1980s and 1990s there was little significant change in the numbers of women in positions of social and political power and authority. However much the numbers of women in paid work changed, there was little sign, in any country, of this change being translated into a greater participation in decision-making on the part of the women. As Lisa Adkins, Annie Phizacklea and Linda McDowell (amongst others) have pointed out, the sexual division of labour in the home still disadvantages women in the workplace. Equally unshiftable was the prevailing discourse on race and the colonial past of the West; the dominant politics of Western governments were those of the endorsement of Western (particularly United States) political hegemony and the marginalization of other cultures and other assumptive worlds. Voices like that of Gayatri Spivak have spoken out about the implicit acceptance of imperialism in Western thinking, and its continuing heritage in the structure of relations between North and South.[37] For women, of whatever colour, this relationship remains crucial, since without recognition of its existence it is impossible to de-construct our national identities in ways which make it possible to re-construct alternative politics. As Avtar Brah has recently argued:

> It is crucial to make it explicit that racism is always a gendered phenomenon.... Not only are men and women from one racialized group differentiated from their counterparts in another racialized group, but the male from a subordinate group may be racialized through the attribution of 'feminine qualities', or the female may be represented as embodying 'male' qualities.[38]

The quotation, and the sources to which the author refers (Carby, bell hooks, Ware, Hall, Lorde et al.) all demonstrate the 'new politics' of feminism in the 1990s. The exposure of the sexism and racism of both the public and the private worlds, which was the dominant theme of the 1970s, has gradually been replaced by an acceptance of the assumption that the two worlds are linked. Feminism has made the connection between the public and the private which Mary Wollstonecraft, in 1792, argued was crucial to any political project. What is now clear is how deep resistance is to this connection, since the radical, and de-stabilizing implications have not been lost on conservative critics. It is to those implications which we shall turn in the following chapter.

43

3
Engendering Knowledge

Towards the end of her life, Simone de Beauvoir became increasingly engaged in feminist politics and party to feminist discussions about language and the construction of knowledge.[1] The *grande dame* of European feminism had been largely distant from organized feminism (such as it was) in France in the 1950s and 1960s, but as 'second wave' feminism became an increasingly vocal part of French politics in the 1970s, so de Beauvoir was rediscovered (or in some cases discovered for the first time) by younger women. The author of *The Second Sex* was turned to for advice and elucidation about the situation of women.

But what was revealing about the exchanges between de Beauvoir and younger feminists was the depth of difference between the generations in terms of an understanding of the world. De Beauvoir was no stranger to radical politics (and through her relationship with Sartre had been involved in them for a significant part of her adult life) but her conception of politics, and of the processes through which we understand the world, seemed to belong to a different world. Educated by and with men, it was clearly apparent that de Beauvoir found great difficulty in abandoning the idea of universalism in knowledge:

that is, she could not accept a version of political or intellectual understanding that allowed for different interpretations of the same phenomenon or the same reality. She certainly believed in competing understandings of the world (and given her background as an existential philosopher could scarcely have done otherwise) but what she systematically maintained was that there is a single truth that can be achieved – not for de Beauvoir the feminist understanding of 'women's language' or 'men's knowledge'. For de Beauvoir these terms, and these identifications, would simply re-enforce the division of the intellectual (and the social) world into that of men and that of women. Her vision, and her goal, was to challenge universal, Western knowledge by another version of universalism.[2] Hence, of course, the extraordinary coherence of *The Second Sex*, since what de Beauvoir does is to propose, in the place of the old order of women as the passive other, a new order in which woman becomes part of the world of the active other. Woman becomes like man, in order to escape the debilitating and endlessly disempowering impact of femininity as the condition of other-ness. Refusing this condition becomes, for de Beauvoir, the definitive feminist project.

But for the generation of feminists who came to read de Beauvoir in the 1960s and the 1970s it was not femininity that was the problem, but masculinity. Hence the discussion of de Beauvoir here is used to highlight the shift within feminism that took place in the 1960s and the 1970s: put simply, feminism discovered and articulated the power of women and through this new sense of the feminine began to refuse to engage with what was seen as 'male' thought and 'male' knowledge. No longer did women wish to integrate themselves into a male understanding of the world; the male understanding of the world (identified in some quarters as responsible at that time for the bombing of Vietnam and the savage suppression of left-wing governments) was seen as negative and aggressive. The critique went further too than a continuation of feminist pacifism; a Western tradition (represented by Vera Brittain and Virginia Woolf in *Three Guineas*) had always been highly critical of male physical aggression, but the focus of the 1970s was to extend this critique to the very way in which knowledge of the world was constructed. De

Beauvoir exemplified the woman 'made' in male traditions and expectations; a woman who turned her back (both personally and intellectually) on the traditional female experiences of the household and motherhood and embraced wholeheartedly the cause of rationality and intellectual life.

In doing so, de Beauvoir followed in a tradition in the West in which women have seen the most viable route from second-class female status in the adoption of the replication of masculinity. In later life, de Beauvoir was to comment briefly on *The Second Sex* and to argue that men could no longer claim universal authority.[3] But by that point, few men did claim universality: post-Foucault and post the social revolutions of the 1960s and the 1970s the moral and intellectual order of the West became increasingly fragmented. The authority of the great 'grand narratives' of the past (in particular that of Marxism) were fractured and punctured both by new forms of intellectual dissent and political events in Western Europe. Thus in a sense de Beauvoir's very project – of reconstructing femininity in more masculine terms – collapsed in the face of the de-construction of masculinity that was apparent in the 1970s and the 1980s in the West.

But – and it is a very important but as far as feminism is concerned – just as masculinity and traditional forms of male authority were de-constructed and challenged by the social and intellectual changes of the 1970s, men, in literal terms of human male persons, are the academics and the intellectual and political gate-keepers of the West in terms of the way in which knowledge is constructed and reproduced. Men remain the great majority of academics, just as they remain the sex with the greater public power and public visibility. Yet at the same time, what they exercise power over is an increasingly pluralistic knowledge, constructed out of diverse experiences and diverse cultures. In some subjects, of course, the connections between gender and subject matter remain opaque: mathematics and statistics do not easily lend themselves to feminist (or indeed masculinist) interpretations. On the other hand, in history, literature, sociology and psychology the issue of gender and gender relations has become an inherent part of those (and other) subjects.

We can explore the ways in which 'knowledge', hopefully a

general, rather than specifically academic term, has been constructed and re-constructed through two themes that have proved a fertile ground for feminist discussion. In the first place, what has been raised is the issue of language, and the very means by which we articulate our understanding of the world in which we live. For de Beauvoir, and for many Anglo-American writers, the issue of language has never been crucial. English is not a grammatically gendered language and few Anglo-Saxons have shown much interest in the issue of gender and the structure of their language, even though intense interest has been raised about the meaning of individual words, and Dale Spender was amongst those who raised the issue of 'Man-Made' Language.[4] But for French writers in the 1960s and 1970s the issue of language became crucial: influenced by Lacan and Derrida, Luce Irigaray, Monique Wittig and Hélène Cixous argued for the rejection of phallocentric language and the construction of a language which could reflect the reality of female desire.[5] The texts that have had the most disruptive presence here are those of *Les Guérillères* by Monique Wittig (published in 1969), Hélène Cixous' *Le Rire de la Méduse* (published in 1975) and Luce Irigaray's essay *This Sex which is not One* (published in 1977).[6]

In order to place these pivotal texts (and the ideas and debates that they have inspired) a diversion in intellectual history is necessary. All the writers mentioned above are informed by psycho-analysis; their position is not – like de Beauvoir – anti psycho-analysis *per se*, but critical of what they see as the phallic emphasis of Freudian psycho-analysis. What they all accept (and this is very much the case for many feminist writers) is the theory of the unconscious, and the theoretical distinctions that this makes possible between the material and the symbolic worlds of individuals. Feminists have often dissented from other aspects of Freud's work (in particular his ideas about penis-envy, the construction of heterosexuality as maturity and the nature of relations between child, father and mother) but there has emerged a general (although not exclusive) acceptance of his ideas about the role, and extent, of fantasy in human emotional experience. Indeed, familiarity with psycho-analysis has become, from the 1970s onwards (particularly after Juliet Mitchell's work of recovery of Freud, *Psychoanalysis and Feminism*) almost a *sine qua non* of academic feminism.

This psycho-analytic literacy within feminism has not, however, stopped at Freud. A major and significant influence has been that of various post-Freudians, in particular the French analyst Jacques Lacan and the Austrian analyst Melanie Klein. (Indeed, as Janet Sayers has pointed out women analysts – Melanie Klein, Hélène Deutsch, Anna Freud and Karen Horney – did much to locate the central dilemma and dynamics of a child's development in terms of its mother rather than its father.)[7] Of these two writers it is Lacan who has been of particular importance in the development of the ways in which women writers (the term feminist is too problematic here) conceptualize language and representation.

Lacan's work is notoriously difficult and complex, and much of the understanding of it can be traced to its translation and discussion by Juliet Mitchell and Jacqueline Rose.[8] In their work, and in their work on Lacan, what they have done is to emphasize Lacan's theory of the phallus as the universal signifier, as the literal representation of the law of the father and as the prime signifier of desire. Janet Sayers, in *Sexual Contradictions*, has summarized the position of Lacan thus:

> Women and men, says Lacan, constitute the phallus the prime signifier of their desire in so far as they recognize this patriarchal law.... This imagined identity is only disrupted, argues Lacan, by the castration complex, by the child's discovery that the phallus is 'absent in the mother'.[9]

What occurs, therefore, in all children is a primary identification with the phallus, which is seen as the active force in the construction of language and culture, in that all is seen in terms of its phallic presence or absence. For Lacanians, and for feminists influenced by Lacan, terms such as 'woman' or 'lesbian' have little or no meaning in that they are constructed around a form of desire that cannot be represented because it has no phallic form. It is this issue of woman, and woman's sexual desire, as constructed around the presence/absence of the masculine, that formed the central issue of *The Sex which is not One* by Irigaray.

This theme – of the impossibility of representing the feminine – is further taken up and elaborated by the French writer and psycho-analyst Julia Kristeva. What unites Kristeva with Cixous, Irigaray and Wittig (and with the tradition of Lacan) is the assertion that women cannot be represented. In a famous interview in *Tel Quel*, published in 1974, Kristeva asserted that:

> In 'woman' I see something that cannot be represented, something that is not said, something above and beyond nomenclatures and ideologies.[10]

And, in the same interview, she also said:

> The belief that 'one is a woman' is almost as absurd and obscurantist as the belief that 'one is a man'. I say 'almost' because there are still many goals which women can achieve: freedom of abortion and contraception, day-care centres for children, equality on the job etc. Therefore, we must use 'we are women' as a slogan or advertisement for our demands. On a deeper level, however, a woman cannot 'be', it is something which does not even belong in the order of *being*. It follows that a feminist practice can only be negative, at odds with what already exists so that we may say 'that's not it' and 'that's still not it'.[11]

Kristeva (like Irigaray, Wittig and Cixous) has been an enormously influential writer both in France and elsewhere. Unlike Lacan, however, she has never avoided a discussion of the material world, and the article that is mentioned above, that contains her well-known assertion of the impossibility of representing the feminine, also contains a very full account of family reforms in China and the implications for women of policies designed by a socialist state for their explicit emancipation. In this, her work is closer to that of many North American writers on women and knowledge, because they, like Kristeva, have attempted to unite an understanding and a theoretical position on the construction of the symbolic world with an understanding of the part played in the material world by the symbolic. The key concept around which feminists have worked in this area is that of 'nature' and it is to the understanding of this idea, and its relationship to knowledge, that psycho-analysis has so fully contributed.

The essential issue around which feminist debates on nature are organized is that expressed by de Beauvoir when she wrote that 'woman is made not born.'[12] As endless commentators have pointed out, this opened up the possibility of demonstrating that women – as feminine beings – are the product of socialization. Numerous studies were conducted, in this framework, to show the impact of child-rearing practices in producing 'masculine' boys and 'feminine' girls.[13] Indeed, the spirit of these studies continues in accounts of educational processes that are said to be based on assumptions about appropriate male and female behaviour. But – and the but is produced by psycho-analysis – other traditions suggest that biological difference is such as to render gender differentiation absolutely inevitable. Against 'woman is made not born' we therefore have to set 'biology is destiny' and confront the a-historical and a-cultural absolutes to which Lacan, Kristeva et al. draw our attention.

Unpicking what is natural and what is social is, of course, an ancient minefield, and a minefield that it is hazardous as well as pointless to traverse in search of final answers. But what feminism has achieved in this area is the very considerable feat of re-examining what we think of, in the West, as knowledge. The connection with Lacan (and others) here is that this is a crucial concept to investigate given the association that has always been made between knowledge and power. When psycho-analysis was re-discovered by feminism in the 1970s it gave women a framework through which they could explore the metaphorical and the symbolic in social and intellectual life as well as the literal. Thus what came to be included in the study of the social world was the idea of exactly what 'knowledge' represents: in one sense, the literal, 'knowledge' is exactly what it claims to be – a particular cluster of information about a phenomenon. But in another sense – and this was the sense explored by the work of psycho-analytically influenced feminists in the 1970s – 'knowledge' also exists to maintain and represent certain forms of domination of the world. Since knowledge of our body is the very first knowledge that any of us acquire, it is apparent why the body, and the discovery of the body, has such a fundamental place in feminist literature. Hence, too, the common cause with Freud, since feminists, like Freud and Freudian analysts, accept that it is through our bodies, and the relationship of our bodies to those of others, that we first acquire knowledge of the world.

Thus the dispute over what kind of knowledge we acquire about our bodies, and our 'nature', can be seen to have such a pivotal importance in the construction of knowledge. The enormous, and lasting, appeal of Irigaray, Cixous and Wittig is that they suggest a knowledge of the nature of the feminine and femininity that is radically different from previous understandings, understandings always located in difference from the male. Hence knowing the female body, and the nature of the feminine has assumed such a central part in recent feminism. Adrienne Rich, well known for her critique of male-centred language and literature has put the issue in this way:

> I am really asking whether women cannot begin, at last, to think through the body, to connect what has been so cruelly disguised – our great mental capacities, hardly used; our highly developed tactile sense; our genius for close observation; our complicated pain-enduring, multipleasured physicality.... The repossession by women of our bodies will bring far more essential changes to society than the seizing of the means of production by workers. The female body has been both territory and machine, virgin wilderness to be exploited and assembly-line turning out life. We need to imagine a world in which every woman is the presiding genius of her own body. In such a world women will truly create new life, bringing forth not only children (if and as we choose) but the visions and the thinking, necessary to sustain, console and alter human existence – a new relationship to the universe.[14]

This passage is quoted at length because it captures a great deal of the visionary quality of the claims made by Rich about the possibilities inherent in the re-knowing, and the re-ordering of knowledge, about the female body. Rich's assertion – that repossessing the female body is more socially radical than the social re-organization of production has been widely echoed, by writers such as Mary Daly.[15] In this radical feminist response to what is perceived as male imperialism about the female body we find little that is socially specific, or willing to engage with the complex, and contradictory, relationships of women to men. Indeed, part of the appeal of Rich (and Irigaray and others) for many readers is that they are a-social, and engaging with general patterns of male and female behaviour. Given the universal information that is available about the mutilation and distortion of the female body, the case about the alienation of women from their bodies becomes apparently overwhelming.

But at the same time as many women wrote, in the 1970s, about the global patterns and manifestations of the degradation of the female body, others came to examine, and to note, the differences in these patterns and the changes that have occurred, both within cultures and between cultures. Thus just as Mary Daly, Robin Morgan and Gayle Rubin (amongst others) began to articulate powerful arguments about the universal alienation of women from their bodies (and the subjection of those bodies to male interests) so others – in anthropology, sociology and history – began to construct the case that suggested that far from a universal pattern of absolute control of women by men, there was (and is) a pattern of universal *contest* around the female body.[16]

What is fascinating about these debates, and arguments, is that it is overwhelmingly the female body that has received attention. Little has been said to suggest that men are alienated from their bodies by women, although there are shelves of books (which have a long history) about the alienation of men from their emotional and intellectual lives. Gay men have written of the pressures on them to become heterosexual but there is generally an acceptance that these pressures come as much from men as from women. The history of sexuality, which has been re-written since the 1960s and the impact of Foucault on social and intellectual history, has largely been written in terms that assume that men (albeit heterosexual men) have been in control of the writing of their own sexual and social history. The general assumption is that women have not, and that since the late sixteenth century, women's relationship to their bodies has been defined in terms of a changing and – to women – detrimental construction of the idea of 'nature'.

It is this concept of 'nature' and its changing meaning that has proved so richly interesting to feminist historians. Essentially, what these historians have argued is that the rise of science in

Europe shifted the understanding of our human relationship to Nature. Nature, once both a benevolent and autocratic force, became a force, a being, to be controlled. Control over nature, and natural phenomena, was of course as ancient as civilization itself, but the difference initiated in the sixteenth and seventeenth centuries lay in the new possibilities for the absolute control and understanding of nature offered by science. To take a fictional example: in Mary Shelley's *Frankenstein*, it is a man who seeks to create life, although he does so when embittered and grief-stricken by the losses that Nature can inflict. Women, as Shelley knew only too well, die in childbirth, but their ability to bear children, and create life, remains inherently superior to the creative powers of men. Technology, as Mary Shelley's novel makes clear (and makes clear at precisely that point in history when Europe is about to experience a massive technological revolution) is inherently different from the powers of Nature. As Frankenstein cries out in horror against the forces of the Enlightenment world: 'Man, how ignorant art thou in thy pride of wisdom.'[17]

Mary Shelley took up, in fiction, the issues that her mother, Mary Wollstonecraft, had raised in *A Vindication of the Rights of Woman*. Mary Wollstonecraft did not explicitly deal with the issue of the changing relationship of women and men to knowledge arising out of the Enlightenment, but *A Vindication* is an appeal for the education of women and an argument for women to be included in what is becoming apparent as the centrality of organized knowledge to social power. It is the recognition (by the end of the eighteenth century) that access to coherent, ordered, formalized and institutional knowledge is crucially important that led women throughout Europe to begin to demand equal access to the universities. But as feminist historians of the seventeenth and eighteenth centuries have now suggested, by the time women were allowed access to institutional knowledge, the *form* of that knowledge had been established and regulated by men. For example, in her account of gender and the rise of modern science, Londa Schiebinger has argued that in the late seventeenth and early eighteenth centuries there was no broad agreement that women did not belong in science as practitioners; however, by the early nineteenth century patterns of exclusion (both ideological and institutional) had led to the general assumption that women did not 'belong' in science.[18] Throughout the nineteenth (and indeed the twentieth) century, women then had to fight and argue their way back into science – and a scientific epistemology and community that they had had little or no part in constructing.

Londa Schiebinger's book was published in 1989, and as such is part of the re-discovery that occurred throughout the 1970s and 1980s of science, and issues connected with it, by feminists. In one sense, science and the scientific community, was all too easy a target for feminists, since in numerical terms it virtually excluded women. Moreover, as Ann Sayre's biography of Rosalind Franklin made all-too-apparent, the professional place of women in science was deeply uncomfortable. The title of the biography, *Rosalind Franklin and DNA: A Vivid View of What it is Like to be a Gifted Woman in an Especially Male Profession* suggests precisely the thesis of the book, although it cannot adequately convey the humiliation and marginalization endured by Rosalind Franklin in her professional life with Crick and Watson. Ann Sayre's biography was published in 1975 and other women (notably Alice Rossi) had by that time documented the virtual absence of women from science.[19] At the same time, another tradition was beginning to develop – represented most fully in the work of Hilary Rose, Sandra Harding and Donna Haraway – around the issue not just of the literal presence (or absence) of women in science but the wider absence of the 'feminine' and – crucially and centrally – the relationship between the absence of women/femininity and the findings and conclusions of science. Put most simply, what these, and other women argued, was that the *questions* that science identified as important were determined by the construction of the social world in which men occupied the public, and women the private, space. The thesis of Rose et al. is that intellectual structures are affected by gendered social divisions; to argue, therefore, for 'abstract' knowledge is to argue for something that does not exist. Sandra Harding, discussing Hilary Rose in *The Science Question in Feminism* puts the argument thus:

Hilary Rose . . . has developed the argument that it is in the thinking and practices of women scientists . . . that we can detect the
outlines of a distinctively feminist theory of knowledge. Its
distinctiveness is to be found in the way its concepts of the
knower, the world to be known, and processes of coming to know
reflect the unification of manual, mental, and emotional ('hand,
brain, and heart') activity characteristic of women's work more
generally. This epistemology not only stands in opposition to the
Cartesian dualisms – intellect vs. body, and both vs. feeling and
emotion – that underlie Enlightenment and even Marxist visions of
science but also grounds the possibility of a 'more complete materialism, a truer knowledge' than that provided by either paternal
discourse.[20]

Thus Sandra Harding recognized, as did others, that the force of
Rose's argument (and historical material such as that provided by
Ann Sayre) was the assertion that an understanding of the implications of the *female* condition was essential to the understanding of modern science. Studies such as that by Schiebinger could
show that before the institutionalization of science (and indeed of
knowledge) and the development of its professional structure,
women could more easily contribute to its work because formal
barriers and qualifications were few. Once these were established,
however, and this was the case as much for any academic discipline, then women – ideologically constructed in terms of a discourse and set of practices around femininity – were inevitably
excluded. As women found in the nineteenth century, entry to the
universities and the professions was hotly contested ground, in
which much of the debate was organized around ideas about the
'nature' of women's intellect.

But what Sandra Harding also suggested about Rose's argument is that a part of the problem with it is the acceptance of
much of the Enlightenment project of science in which, as
Harding puts it:

Enlightenment thinkers refused to detach women's and men's
social roles from the description and depiction of physiological
differences.[21]

Hence an argument that explains the nature of science by

reference to gender divisions is, in part, a continuation of a tradition in which sexual divisions, and more importantly, sexual differences, inform every aspect of our thinking. Many feminist writers about science and medicine would therefore conclude (and here the work of Ludmilla Jordanova on eighteenth- and nineteenth-century biomedical science in France and England is an excellent instance) that it would seem to be impossible for scientists to think, without thinking about sexuality and sexual imagery. As Jordanova suggests:

> science and medicine as activities were associated with sexual metaphors which were clearly expressed in designating nature as a woman to be unveiled, unclothed and penetrated by masculine science.[22]

The evidence that has been collected by Ludmilla Jordanova, Evelyn Fox Keller and many others has demonstrated the ways in which science, and scientific rationality, are suffused with sexual concerns and sexual images.[23] To Julia Kristeva and Luce Irigaray this would hardly constitute a surprise, since their understanding of the world assumes that language and construction of knowledge are closely linked to sexuality. But to the scientific and academic community, these ideas are heretical, since what the communities are constructed around is a belief in 'scientific' and 'objective' theory. Although there is a coherent critique of this belief by men, the critique is largely based on political criticism of the Western academy, a criticism that sees much of what passes for 'knowledge' being the legitimation of the industrial-capitalist state. It is not, therefore, that we should fall into the trap of assuming either the hegemony or the unity of the 'male' academy; any student of any subject can point to numbers of male critiques of that subject. But what feminists have done with the tradition of the critique of knowledge is to take the more radical stance of attacking not just the conclusions, the arguments and the content of knowledge, but the very way in which knowledge is constructed. Part of that critique centres around language, and the way in which male, or masculinist, language organizes ideas into forms that exclude the female and the feminine. But an equally important part of the critical project of feminism has been a discussion of what Elizabeth Fee and Evelyn Fox Keller identified in the early 1980s as the 'tyranny of facts'.[24] It was not that these authors opposed in any absolute or literal sense the possibility of the existence of clear and unambiguous statements about the world, but that they proposed a way of thinking about the world, and natural phenomena, which did not impose absolutes upon relationships and realities that were often complex and contradictory.

What is interesting about the chronology of the developments of a feminist critique of science and rational/objective inquiry is that it emerged in the late 1970s and early 1980s at the point when, particularly in the United States, feminism was beginning to establish itself as an academic discipline. Alice Rossi had asked the question 'Women in Science: Why so Few?' in 1965, but the implications of the question had not been taken up until later. Indeed, in the late 1960s and early 1970s much feminist energy was concentrated in securing entry for women to the ranks of the professional academy; issues about childcare, maternity leave and direct and explicit discrimination against women were central to feminist concerns, and more complex questions about the inherently gendered form and content of knowledge were largely ignored or marginal. But in the early 1970s Kate Millett published *Sexual Politics* and in doing so issued a challenge to orthodox and conventional assumptions that was to be taken up in contexts other than those of the study of English literature and literary criticism. Millett's book was an enormous commercial success, and its central thesis, that Anglo-Saxon literature was essentially misogynist was taken up by women writers of fiction and non-fiction. The publication of *Sexual Politics* thus encouraged not just the development of further studies of literary criticism, it also encouraged and supported the already burgeoning tradition of women's fictional writing. Obviously, fiction by women was as old as the Western novel itself, but the 'new' fiction by women prioritized women, and women's experiences, in a way that shifted many of the expectations about the vision of fiction. Erica Jong's *Fear of Flying*, Lisa Alther's *Kinflicks* and – slightly later – Maya Angelou's *I Know Why the Caged Bird Sings* and Alice Walker's *The Color Purple*, were just a few of the novels by women that suggested an *explicit* new standpoint in fiction.

Thus once a new standpoint was established, or being established, in fiction, it was only a short step to considering a new standpoint in other subjects as well. The universal cry went up that what women and men were being taught was men's history, men's psychology, men's science and so on. It was then no longer a question about the literal absence of women from the academy (and science) but their metaphorical absence as well: where and how and by whom were women considered in the academic syllabus. The answer was generally nowhere; a few great works by women academics were produced and re-discovered (such as Ivy Pinchbeck on *Women Workers in the Industrial Revolution*) but on the whole the project of the academy was found to be sadly deficient in a discussion of women.

To remedy this state of affairs, women who were feminists and academics began to turn to their own disciplines with a new critical verve. The expansion of higher education in the West in the 1970s (an expansion that made possible the entry of large numbers of white, middle-class women undergraduates into Western universities) had also seen the recruitment of a number of women as academics: these women did not always bring with them feminist values but many did, and were to integrate feminist politics into academic understanding. Thus the personal links between the women's movement and the Western academy of the 1970s were very strong, if often contested. (One example of exactly how close these links were was *Sexual Politics* itself, which was originally written as a doctoral thesis). The results of the fusion of these two traditions could be seen from the mid-1970s onwards; some disciplines were more obvious, and accessible, targets than others but by the beginning of the 1980s few academic subjects and practices had escaped feminist scrutiny.

The natural sciences were to prove one of the more alluring, if more resistant, subjects for re-evaluation. Of the authors mentioned above, Sandra Harding began her work in the mid-1970s, whilst Londa Schiebinger belonged to a younger generation. Hilary Rose had long been a sociologist of science before turning her attention to the gender relations of the subject; Donna

Haraway, like Sandra Harding, belonged to the generation of women who took up academic jobs in the 1970s. All these women – though more so in the United States than in Great Britain – had to deal with opposition to their work, and particularly opposition that took the form of the refusal of tenure and/or promotion. To work in Women's Studies, or to write feminist accounts of science, was often not seen as academically significant or acceptable in the same way as more conventional approaches. Thus many feminist academics faced, in the 1970s, professional marginalization for their work, whilst at the same time receiving considerable praise and confirmation from women critics and readers.

As feminist critics of science began to uncover the history and assumptions of science, and to identify its masculinist practices, so women working in psychology and sociology turned to their subjects to examine the discussion of women. As in the case of science, the 'natural' and 'nature' came to figure largely in the debates, if only because so much seemed to depend upon the acceptance of 'natural' sexual divisions in the world. The medieval rhyme 'When Adam delved and Eve span, who was then the gentleman?' has always been widely quoted by social radicals, but it is only more recently that the inherent sexual conservatism of the rhyme might even have been noticed. But in the 1970s it was noticed, and what was assumed to be 'natural' and part of the 'natural' order of the world came to be regarded with deep suspicion, if not hostility, by feminists.

The issue around which much of the debate in the social sciences was organized was that of the sexual division of labour. In short, feminists began to ask questions about the assumed, 'natural' responsibility of women to care for children, the aged and the infirm and at the same time be just as 'naturally' excluded from anything corresponding to real social or political power. Thus a new understanding and vocabulary was developed by feminist social scientists that identified 'women's work', the 'caring professions', 'unpaid domestic labour', 'the double shift' and other manifestations of the apparently 'natural' social division of labour. In a way that was to have immensely radical and far-reaching implications outside the academy, women collectively questioned their role as the providers of domestic care and emotional nurturance. Throughout the West a generation of women identified what they saw as unpaid, and essentially un-free, labour in the home.

The participants in the domestic labour debate were many. The actual reality of domestic work (childcare, housework and so on) was first documented by Hannah Gavron and Betty Friedan in the 1960s, but that documentary evidence was further extended by Ann Oakley's famous studies of housework in the 1970s and the accounts by feminist historians (for example Sally Alexander, Sheila Rowbotham and Joan Scott) of the infinite variety of work that women had always done.[25] If the emphasis of this work was on the demonstration of the extent of women's work, its theoretical basis evolved in conjunction with the contemporary debates on patriarchy and the political economy of domestic labour. 'Materialist' feminism took many, different, forms but there was a consensus, however fragile, that women within the household made a contribution significantly higher than their reward. Marxist feminists joined battle over the meaning of the term 'surplus value', and the work of Marx, and Engels, was re-discovered as a rich source of both theoretical inspiration and theoretical sexism. Irene Bruegel and Veronica Beechey, for example, developed highly sophisticated accounts of women's paid work within this context.[26] In *Patriarchal Precedents* (which was published in 1983) Rosalind Coward wrote a comprehensive indictment of the work of Marx and Darwin, an indictment based largely on a critique of the way in which these pivotal figures, unthinkingly or otherwise, refused to question the sexual division of labour and with it a whole structure of sexual relations. It was not, as Rosalind Coward and other women writers sympathetic to Marx wrote, that he was actually in favour of what he described as the 'bourgeois family'. Indeed, Marx – and even more so Engels – was much in favour of the entry of women into 'paid wage labour' as a pre-requisite for their emancipation. But they could not see beyond the categories of male and female, public and private, to construct a social order that did not assume that the emancipation of women lay in the replication of male patterns.

It was that nineteenth- (and indeed) twentieth-century thesis that men/the masculine represented normality that was gradually eroded by feminism and feminist academics in the 1970s and 1980s. As Coward and many others pointed out, many radicals (of both sexes) in the nineteenth and twentieth centuries could only see the emancipation of women in a liberation towards masculinity. And there was little reason to question this: since women were virtually not citizens, had little education and only unreliable control of their fertility, it was difficult to perceive emancipation within the feminine condition. The very cry of women throughout the nineteenth century was Jane Eyre's cry from the battlements of Thornfield Hall:

> Women are supposed to be very calm generally: but women feel just as men feel; they need exercise for their faculties, and a field for their efforts, as much as their brothers do; they suffer from too rigid a restraint, too absolute a stagnation, precisely as men would suffer.[27]

But Jane Eyre's cry, as other women were also to point out, was not just about access to the masculine condition, it was about access to the privileged masculine condition, and that meant, and means, the white, middle class.

It was this undisclosed, and unspoken, agenda that was to become – and remain – a deeply contentious issue within feminism. Socialist feminist historians (those mentioned above and others including Anna Davin, Linda Gordon and Barbara Taylor) had demonstrated the difficulty of assuming a single feminist vision or programme.[28] Working-class women, they argued, might well have wishes to stay out of the labour force rather than be in it, since what was not available to them, unlike middle-class women, was professional or white collar employment. Equally, black women contested the very perimeters of white feminism as a whole: Hazel Carby in Britain and Angela Davis in the United States were amongst those who raised difficult questions about the different degrees of privilege and/or exploitation made possible through social systems that were based not just on social divisions, but on racial divisions as well.[29] Again, black feminists could demonstrate the conservative impact of ideas about 'nature' on the lives of women. In this case the women in question were non-white, but assumed to be, in crucial ways, different from white women. To take another example from *Jane Eyre*: just as the white, middle-class Jane Eyre cries for her freedom, she hears the cries from the attic of the 'mad' Mrs Rochester; a woman who is not just socially disruptive because of her uncertain temper but who is arguably disruptive and unstable precisely because she is what Rochester refers to as 'Creole'.

Such is the imaginative richness of *Jane Eyre* that it contains not just a critique of Victorian expectations about women, but an equally passionate – if much less explicit – critique of Victorian attitudes to the Empire and the entire project of imperialism. Rochester, by his own confession, is only concerned to exploit the West Indies. (In this he follows the fictional path of Sir Thomas Bertram in Jane Austen's *Mansfield Park*, but unlike Sir Thomas he extends his social relationships to include the local inhabitants.) In *Jane Eyre*, St John Rivers is equally concerned to subdue the colonies, only in his case not by economic exploitation but by the word of the Bible. Both men are thwarted in the absolute fulfilment of their projects by women: Rochester's wife goes 'mad' (and goes mad in a way that women writers from Jean Rhys to Elaine Showalter and Sandra Gilbert and Susan Gubar have found endlessly and richly fascinating) and Jane Eyre refuses to become an accomplice to St John Rivers's colonizing exploits.[30] Thus although separated by race and class, Jane Eyre and Bertha Rochester share a position of *refusal* to male interests that makes them both inherently subversive.

However, the fictional unity of Jane Eyre and Bertha Rochester has yet to be replicated by a corresponding sense of unity of purpose or understanding between white and non-white feminists. The literature on non-white women has grown enormously since the 1970s, and the women who have spoken for non-white women (in particular Audré Lorde from the 1970s to her untimely death in 1994 and Gayatri Spivak in the 1980s and 1990s) have become icons of feminism. In different ways both have pointed out the problems faced by feminism in constructing a universal feminism: in just the same way as the male and masculinity was de-constructed as the universal norm, so feminism has to be de-constructed to allow for difference and diversity between women, quite as much as between women and men. The two words 'difference' and 'diversity' have thus become synonymous with feminism in the 1990s.

But no account of the history of feminism in the 1970s and the 1980s, and the systematic critique of a 'natural' order of sexual difference that it bequeathed, would be complete without a reference to the work of Carol Gilligan on the difference between the moral reasoning of women and men. The crucial work on this issue was *In a Different Voice*, first published in the United States in 1982, and resulting from research on a group of adolescent girls and their attitude to abortion. Essentially, Gilligan took issue with the work of the psychologist Lawrence Kohlberg, who had argued (following Freud) that women had less developed moral reasoning than men, and the reasons for this lay in the psychological impact of biological difference. Kohlberg's book had become accepted as orthodoxy in psychology, and as Carol Gilligan pointed out, the implications of the idea were that women were unable to think objectively or to abandon the particular in the light of general principles. What Gilligan did with this argument (and the literature on her work is now considerable) was to suggest that women's moral reasoning is not deficient – in terms relative to that of men – but is different.[31] The strength of women's moral reasoning, she argues, is precisely that it does not assert the general at the cost of the particular, nor seek an absolute standard that may have little relationship to reality.

As suggested, debate about this thesis continues, and continues within the disciplines of law and theology quite as much as in psychology. But it also has had repercussions in the oldest of the academic subjects, namely philosophy, in which assumptions about the different natures of women and men have been enshrined, both implicitly and explicitly, since Aristotle. The heritage to Western philosophy of the Greeks is hardly contentious, what is more contentious and is now raised by feminist philosophers, is exactly how far that heritage is flawed by its bias towards the male. In opening up the debate about morality, what Carol Gilligan also did was to encourage women in philosophy to examine their subject, and to examine their subject for partiality. In 1983 Alison Jagger articulated this vision thus:

63

Women's subordinate status means that, unlike men, women do not have an interest in mystifying reality and so are likely to develop a clearer and more trustworthy understanding of the world. A representation of reality from the standpoint of women is more objective and unbiased than the prevailing representations that reflect the standpoint of men.

The concept of women's standpoint also provides an interpretation of what it is for a theory to be comprehensive. It asserts that women's social position offers them access to aspects or areas of reality that are not easily accessible to men. . . . The standpoint of women reveals more of the universe, human or non-human, than the standpoint of men.[32]

Subsequent discussions by women in philosophy have modified and questioned the claims made by Jagger. But what has not changed is the recognition by women that philosophy in the 1990s is not the same subject as it was in the 1970s, and it is not the same in ways other than the conventional, and accepted, development of an academic subject. It is not the same because – as for the social sciences and the humanities in general – universalism is a contested concept. Furthermore, the impact of theories of de-construction have been such as to render impossible any continuation of general ideas about 'citizens' or 'people'. The radical shifts in our understanding of language suggested by Irigaray, Kristeva et al. have come to involve shifts in the very institutional and academic structures created by language.

4

Representation

The relationship between the literal and the symbolic is not, as any student of literature and the visual arts knows, anything other than complex. Yet acknowledging the complexity of the relationship, and the theoretical implications of the relationship, has often been difficult for literary and artistic critics. Feminist critics have been, in this respect, no less apt than other critics to follow diverse ideas about the relationship. Indeed, in the early days of second wave feminism a great deal of feminist literary criticism took literally the words and meanings of the printed page: a novel with a female central character was described as 'feminist' and complex meanings in fiction were a thing of the future of feminist criticism.[1]

What has now emerged, is a feminist literary criticism that is rich in its readings of texts and a major contemporary force (arguably *the* major force) in the 'reading' of literature. In twenty-five years, therefore, feminist literary criticism has come to achieve a theoretical impact on our reading of both the printed word and the visual image. Numerous detailed studies demonstrate the validity and the range of the approach. The key that has unlocked this treasure house of re-interpretation is that of psycho-analysis: Freud's suggestion that we should distinguish between fantasy and reality – whilst allowing that fantasy can be reality just as reality can be fantasy – has allowed women writers to review the traditional ways in which literature is read.

In order to situate the impact of feminism on academic literary criticism it has to be remembered that, in the 1960s, literary (and visual arts) criticism in British and North American universities contained diverse theoretical traditions. Highly influential was the work of F.R. Leavis, who with his wife Q.D. Leavis argued for an aesthetic of tradition, which gives 'meaning to the past'.[2] Leavis, like many other critics of this period from different political persuasions, was centrally concerned to oppose the literary products of popular and consumer culture. An explicit example of this view was Q.D. Leavis's *Fiction and the Reading Public*, a work that attacked developing genres of popular fiction such as detective fiction and romantic novels. In this hostility to class-related diversity in fiction bourgeois critics such as Leavis shared the same view as Marxist critics such as Georg Lukács: to both, what was at stake was a dilution of critical standards and the disappearance of the 'high' art of Europe beneath a tidal wave of largely North American values and products.[3] At the time when Leavis and Lukács were writing, cultural studies, indeed the study of popular culture in all, was hardly dreamt of in the Western academy.

This confident bourgeois hegemony (whether of the political left or right) was shattered throughout the West by the Second World War and the populist endorsement of mass culture. It took some time for literary critics to come to terms with this new world (and one that included new nations as well as new classes) but by the early 1960s university departments throughout the West were beginning the academic study of popular culture. When Richard Hoggart and Stuart Hall founded the Centre for Contemporary Cultural Studies at the University of Birmingham it became clear that the study of literature would become far more pluralistic than previously allowed.

In retrospect, what is interesting about the debates and discussions that surrounded the establishment of the 'new' English literature syllabus is that it took some time – indeed until the early

1970s – for the *sexual* politics of literary modernism and popular culture to become an issue. It was then only with the publications of feminist literary critics that links were made between modernism in literature, sexual politics and changes in fictional accounts of subjectivity. The key writer of the twentieth century who demonstrates this transition is Virginia Woolf, a novelist who did not so much abolish narrative as suspend it, and whose novels explored not the 'true' nature of individuals but their diverse and contradictory selves. Such an idea was, of course, anathema to the majority of male writers and critics, whose internalized belief in the heroic made it essential that the central characters of the novel should, in some sense, be identifiable. Woolf's resistance to this idea, most forcefully expressed in *Orlando*, was to suggest the exact opposite, that of all things the person is unknowable and impossible to define. Advancing this position then puts the author in a different relation to the characters, in that the author is no longer offering the readers a particular person but is exploring the diversity of a named individual. What this opens up is the possibility of fiction as a theoretical exercise of enormous sophistication, rather than as a story-telling exercise about fixed characters.

A traditional male response to the questioning of fictional certainty can be seen in the critical essays of George Orwell. Although not a professional critic, Orwell's essays on literature were widely cited in critical circles and were a kind of benchmark for many critics.[4] Orwell's loathing of anything associated with either modernity or the Bloomsbury group was well known, and subsequent critics have noted his homophobic fear of anything approaching subjectivity in men. The version of masculinity endorsed in his work was that of men as the agents of socialist history; more complex relationships to the world were not allowed, and women scarcely appeared as characters in his work, let alone believable ones. But the point of citing Orwell here is to demonstrate how white male writers fought to maintain the 'form' of masculinity deemed appropriate: a form that marginalized relations with women, was deeply involved in, yet denied, emotional relationships with men and gave an absolute priority to objective, rather than subjective, reality and experience.

67

Anglo-Saxon male writers were particularly anxious to maintain this version of the male; France produced Marcel Proust, but the United States and Britain in the 1920s, 1930s and 1940s produced figures such as Greene, Hemingway and Faulkner. In drama and poetry, a coded literature of homosexuality emerged (in Terence Rattigan and Tennessee Williams for example) but the possible boundaries of fiction were largely being explored (for example in Henry Miller and earlier D.H. Lawrence) in the explicit depiction of heterosexual relationships.

What feminist critics have made of these writers, and the literary contests of the first half of the twentieth century, has largely been to situate them in terms of the negotiation of gender identity.[5] This in itself was a radical re-reading of literature, since prior to 1970 almost no-one had explicitly discussed the history of fiction in terms of gender politics. Class politics in literature had long been on the agenda, but the idea that gender and sexuality were being fought over and negotiated in the novel and poetry was entirely original.[6] Thus from the 1970s, what emerged from feminism were three main shifts in the understanding of the representation (whether written or visual) of the human condition: first, feminism initiated the discovery and the creation of a 'new' literature – a literature specifically about women. Every user of almost any bookshop (and increasingly many supermarkets) will now be familiar with the green covers of the Virago Modern Classics. This series, established in 1978, had as its organizing principle the publication of hitherto little-known works of fiction. It was not, therefore, that the series was designed to publish new fiction by women but to demonstrate the richness of the tradition of fiction by women. Through the Virago Modern Classics series the women writers who had been marginalized or largely ignored by mainstream male traditions were brought again to the attention of the reading public.

But the second strand to the extension of the boundaries of fiction was the development of original fiction by women. In the United States, Erica Jong and others became synonymous with the 'new' women's writing. This *genre* was rapidly visible within other national and cultural contexts; in particular black women writers in the United States produced powerful fictional accounts of their own lives and of fictional women. In prose and in poetry, a new women's literature was visible by the 1970s, a literature that used traditional forms and *genres* (the novel and the detective story, for example) to extol a feminist case. As women-writers of fiction were exploring the boundaries and possibilities of the novel, so feminist critics turned to the re-examination of literary history and theories of representation.

It is in these two areas that feminism can, in retrospect, be seen to have had a marked impact on academic understanding. No Women's Studies course is complete without some discussion of representation, and the history of the development of the area offers an interesting example of the ways in which academic paradigms change. Put simply, the history was as follows: in the first place (in historical terms the early 1970s) the main concern and Women's Studies in literature was to demonstrate that women were there at all, and that they had played a part in literature and the arts. This was similar to the project of the Virago Classics and, in another context – that of socialist literary criticism and the identification of the working class in fiction – a project of discovery and intellectual archaeology. Thus the first major emphasis with literature and the arts in the 1970s was on the demonstration of the existence of women writers and artists, previously ignored or marginalized by the canon. Women as victims – of male exploitation and misrepresentation – was a key theme in these early years.[7]

The conditions that made possible male participation in the arts, and female participation difficult, were summed up by Germaine Greer in *The Obstacle Race*, a discussion of women artists hitherto little known either to the public or specialist audiences.[8] The book united the two themes of the early engagement of feminism with the arts and literature: a concern with the structural constraints on women's achievements in these areas plus an attack on the standards, the perceptions and the judgements of critical traditions that simply did not perceive the work of women. 'Great' as Greer, and others, pointed out, was always taken for granted as male, and women – whatever the intrinsic value of their work – as secondary or inferior. The idea is initially an attractive one, since it seems to suggest that there is a clear, coherent and consistent tradition within artistic and literary canons that faithfully praises the same great male writers and artists and ignores the rest. Unfortunately, the history of literary and artistic criticism does not bear this out; whilst some figures (and Shakespeare is one such example) have always been performed and played some part in the national literary canon of England, other writers and artists have had much more chequered careers. Kenneth Clark's work on the history of art is just one example of a context in which a conventional male critic cites the considerable shifts that have occurred within the appraisal of male artists; but at no point (even given that his subject involves the female nude) engages with issues of gender politics.[9] Nevertheless, allowing for the inconsistency of dominant traditions should not obscure the considerable consistency of that tradition in suppressing or refusing the work of women. Women artists have clearly been more marginal to the development of painting and drawing than have women writers to fiction; for an explanation we have to look no further than the basic costs involved in each enterprise. If women writers such as Jane Austen could write (and did write) on a dining room table, then had her sister wished to paint or draw she would have been involved in a considerable outlay of funds for basic equipment.

But however different the basic costs involved in art and literature, these were as nothing compared to the difficulty of the resources of time and energy necessary for any kind of creative work. Again, feminist critics pointed out (in the 1970s just as much as they had done for generations) that the majority of women simply did not have time to write or paint, and – at least as important – nobody expected them to have that resource. 'Women's time' as Julia Kristeva was to describe it in one of the most seminal papers of the 1970s, is not time that is seen to belong to women: men 'possess' time in the sense of being able to control their commitments.[10] Women, on the other hand, are commonly seen as a boundless resource in which their every minute is available to others. Little wonder, then, as many feminists have pointed out, that the women who have achieved great distinction in the creative arts are generally both unmarried and childless. Marriage and children were, therefore, the great inhibitors of the development of female talent in the eighteenth and nineteenth centuries.

But just as marriage and children still remain powerful constraints on female achievements in the twentieth century, so we have to add a third – that of the professionalization of many areas of the creative arts – of ways that exclude women. The genesis of the cinema as an art form, the establishment of a professional theatrical establishment in every Western society and in all areas the increased emphasis on professional training and socialization have increased rather than decreased the difficulties women face in gaining entry to, and recognition within, the arts generally. As Janet Woolf has suggested in *Feminine Sentences*:

> The fact that institutionalized knowledge reflects (and also produces) gender inequalities, giving priority to men's areas of knowledge and social life, is connected to the development of the professions since the nineteenth century. The separation of new and distinct disciplines out of earlier more general areas of knowledge was itself the product of the increasing professionalization of work.[11]

This 'professionalization of work' has applied as much to the arts as to other occupations; the implications for women of this development being that they have to negotiate a largely male professional infrastructure in order to work in the cinema, the theatre or publishing and second, and by association, women are often the passive objects – the 'sign' – of institutional and ideological representation by a male cultural establishment. Resistance to this has been fierce and in a number of ways women have contested the ways in which they are represented, not least through writing and creating their own forms of representation. The resistance thus takes the dual form of opposition (through campaigns against pornography or sexism in advertising) and through the creation of specifically feminine (if not feminist) forms of writing and representation. The photography of Jo Spence and Mary Kelly's work on montage (most famously *Post Partum Document*) are just two well-known examples of the determined work by women artists to claim an autonomous female space in representation and subvert what has been described as the 'male gaze'.[12]

The recognition by feminist art and literary critics of the early 1970s of the strength and the dominance of the ideological and cultural construction of women by men led to what can only be described as a seismic shift in cultural and artistic theory. The absence of women writers and artists was hardly a novel theme (Virginia Woolf's *A Room of One's Own* had dealt absolutely specifically with the theme in 1929) but the real shift was the thesis that gender politics were absolutely central to the very project of representation, be it through words or through visual images. No student of English literature anywhere in the West would have read that literature without discovering Jane Austen, Emily and Charlotte Brontë, George Eliot, Mrs Gaskell and Virginia Woolf, but the interpretation of the work of the authors given to generations before 1970 was deeply entrenched in the taken-for-granted assumptions of a male critical establishment. 'Re-reading' English, as it was to be described by Catherine Belsey and others in the 1970s was thus an exercise less in the discovery of literally new authors, but in the recovery of known authors from the grip of conventional certainties.[13] Those certainties involved the absence from critical dialogue of the dynamics of sexual power and of the coded information given by female authors to their readers. To quote Janet Woolf again:

> Lastly, theories of reception have been mobilized to expose the denial to women of a subject position as reader. Jonathan Culler asks what it would be like to read the opening of Thomas Hardy's *The Mayor of Casterbridge* (which deals with a wife-sale) as a woman. Just as art criticism and film criticism have demonstrated the ways in which texts constitute their readers/viewers as male, so feminist literary critics have identified that necessary process which has been called the 'emasculation of the reader' – that is, the need for women, if they are to be competent readers in our culture, to take on the point of view of men.'[14]

This last point can be illustrated over and over again by reference to most of the works of most of the 'great' writers and artists of the Western canon of the visual and literary arts. In a feminist reading, we do not, for example, take for granted quite so easily Anna Karenina's suicide or the rape of Clarissa. What becomes more visible, in a culture literate in both psycho-analysis and in feminism is that in *Anna Karenina* Tolstoy is punishing Anna for her ability (and that of all women) to engage and to incite sexual desire in men. The furious attack on Anna, and the virtual destruction by the author of her moral credibility as a woman, as a mother and as a lover, comes, we might now argue, from the deep rage of a man unable to allow the sexual and indeed the moral powers of women. Equally, the rape of Clarissa, in Richardson's novel, can now be read in terms of the same male fury at the resistance of women to male expectations. Clarissa's death – the first anorexic death in literature – is then no accident but a conscious act of resistance and the tragic assertion of autonomy. It was a male critic – Terry Eagleton – who re-read *Clarissa* in this way, but even in that reading, sympathetic as it is to feminism, the active agency of Clarissa Harlowe is sometimes made inferior to her status as a victim.[15]

Anna Karenina and *Clarissa* are just two examples of the way in which the 'great' literature of the past is now being re-read and re-interpreted, as actively as other women are creating a new culture of and about women. As suggested earlier, the early 1970s saw the publication of works that questioned the male reading of literature: Kate Millett's *Sexual Politics* achieved lasting, and global fame, but there were other texts, by feminists of an earlier generation that also questioned traditional patriarchal readings of literature. Of these Elizabeth Hardwick's *Seduction and Betrayal* and Ellen Moers's *Literary Women* both asserted readings of literature that gave a new priority, indeed centrality, to the views of women. Thus by the mid-1970s, the point was widely established that literature and the visual arts were ripe for re-interpretation, as assuredly as a new feminist creativity was producing the works located in a feminist analysis of gender relations. Reviewing the development of a new feminist criticism in the United States in 1985 Elaine Showalter could point to an established and vital tradition.[16]

But even by that point – and increasingly in the late 1970s and the 1980s – differences within feminist criticism began to appear and began to demonstrate sharp divisions in opinion. Generally, these divisions took the form of those who read literature as a

73

direct expression of social reality (and therefore used literature and the visual arts as resources of information about women) and those who read literature in terms of post-structuralist and psycho-analytic critiques. What was also crucial to the later group – although far from absent in the first – was an understanding of literature and the visual arts within the context of modernism. The congruence of modernism and feminism remarked upon by many critics, was thus a central organizing concept of this perspective and one that was to inform a number of studies, not just of literature and the arts but of the experience of being, and of living, within Western modernity.[17] Again, the intellectual resources used to develop this point were not solely feminist: crucial to the literature on modernity were the works of Walter Benjamin and Georg Simmel, both of whom identified particular aspects of urban life (for example, in Benjamin's case the person of the *flâneur* in the modern city) that were to inform later feminist accounts of city life by writers such as Elizabeth Wilson and Rachel Bowlby.[18]

Thus the experience of modernity was recognized across the feminist range of critical inquiry. Yet within the common boundaries shared by the mutual acknowledgement of this experience and the centrality of women rather than men to critical practice, literary criticism was to see sharp disputes between feminists. These disputes can be best illustrated by reference to three works (a book and two articles) that took issue with ideas within feminist criticism. In chronological order, the articles were Cora Kaplan, on 'Radical Feminism and Literature' (published in 1979) and Ros Coward's 'Are Women's Novels Feminist Novels?' (published in 1980). The text in question was Toril Moi's *Sexual/Textual Politics*, published in 1985. What unites all these publications (whatever the individual differences in emphasis between the authors) is their resistance to the literal use of the term 'woman'. All the writers subscribe to the view that whatever the impact or the meaning of the term 'woman' in material reality, its construction in ideological, and indeed emotional terms, is extremely complex and not reducible to a single meaning. Hence a highly complex critique of the interpretation of the word 'woman' has emerged in literary criticism. On the one hand – and in varying degrees of complexity and theoretical sophistication – are those critics who read the term 'woman' as implying absolute difference from 'man' and those who, on the other hand, read the term as merely an indicator of biological difference, that has to be read in other, metaphorical, terms as well. Crucial to the theoretical position of the latter group is Freud's proposition that sexual identity is inherently unstable and subject to shifts and changes.

So the debates within theories of representation can be seen in terms of opposition between those who interpret 'woman' literally, and those who advance a more metaphorical reading of the term. When Cora Kaplan wrote 'Radical Feminism and Literature' she did so in response to what she described as Kate Millett's highly 'positivistic' reading of literature. Thus:

> The whole of *Sexual Politics* is permeated by a coercive sexual morality, meant to replace those mores inscribed in patriarchy. Typical of the early years of the modern women's movement, it borrows from the sixties alternative ideologies, which in turn reacted against the macho poses of the post-war fifties. It is marked, among other things, by an extreme distaste for the recrudescent sado-mas elements of sexuality, however playfully practised. Surprisingly, it has very rigid notions of sexual health.[19]

Kaplan's critique of *Sexual Politics* became a widely quoted one, and was in part a contribution to the furious debates on sexuality that erupted at Barnard College in the United States in 1982.[20] What Kaplan had done, in effect, was to assert the importance of the complexity of the text, and its right to a reading that would challenge as well as illustrate feminist theory.

This theme – of the difference between texts and their status as independent from imposed theories – was taken up by Ros Coward in the article cited above. In response to suggestions for holiday reading made by Rebecca O'Rourke, Ros Coward argued:

> Because the article simply draws the reader's attention to the multitude of new or reprinted novels it fails to engage with more interesting questions about feminist writings, grouping together such different writers as Michèle Roberts and Stella Gibbons under the

category 'women writers'. It would be difficult to find much in common between these two writers.[21]

And she goes on:

It is just not possible to say that women-centred writings have any necessary relationship to feminism.[22]

There, in a sentence, is the crux of the matter: the rejection of the idea that 'woman' is synonymous with 'feminist' and that the term 'woman' is in itself oppositional. It was this theme that Toril Moi was to develop in *Sexual/Textual Politics*, in large part a critique of what she, like Cora Kaplan, identified as the positivistic tendency in feminist literary criticism in the United States in the 1970s. Beginning by a review of *Sexual Politics* and Mary Ellmann's *Thinking about Women* (both of which get, from Moi, very mixed reviews) she turns to a discussion of what is described as 'Images of Women' criticism. The main point of this chapter is to demonstrate what Moi describes as 'the deep realist bias of Anglo-American feminist criticism', a demonstration that usefully prefaces her subsequent discussion of the work of the feminist literary critics Sandra Gilbert, Susan Gubar, Ellen Moers and Elaine Showalter. Gilbert and Gubar had published, in 1979, *The Madwoman in the Attic: The Woman Writer and the Nineteenth Century Literary Imagination*, whilst Ellen Moers was the author of *Literary Women* (1976) and Elaine Showalter of (most crucially at the time that Moi was writing *Sexual/Textual Politics*) *A Literature of their Own: British Women Novelists from Brontë to Lessing*, which was published in 1977.

The strength of these critics is acknowledged by Moi (even if the terms of the praise, such as 'massive volume' for *The Madwoman in the Attic* suggests endurance rather than critical perception) but the main theme of her argument is that:

The central paradox of Anglo-American feminist criticism is thus that despite its often strong, explicit political engagement, it is *in the end* not quite political enough; not in the sense that it fails to go *far* enough along the political spectrum, but in the sense that its radical analysis of sexual politics still remains entangled with depoliticizing theoretical paradigms.[23]

Thus whilst Moi is more than willing to praise Showalter et al. for their vigorous demonstration of sexual politics in the novel (and particularly in its great age of realism between 1750 and 1930) she has reservations about what she sees as the refusal of Anglo-American critics to engage with humanist and liberal readings of fiction – those readings mentioned earlier in this chapter as central to conventional literary criticism. What this failure to engage leaves undisturbed is, of course, the class politics of the novel and the subversive, and often positively transgressive, attacks on the conventional order and conventional masculinity that are to be found in the work of male, as well as female, authors.

It is this difference of opinion around the boundaries of the transgressive, both in literature and in representation in general, that has fuelled considerable, and considerably heated, feminist debate in the 1980s and 1990s. The point made by Moi was taken up and developed by a number of feminist critics, all of whom were essentially concerned to show the multiplicities of meaning in texts and the importance of reading in ways that allowed the internal ambiguities and contradictions of literature to emerge. The traditions that informed this development were consistently those of psycho-analysis and of French feminism. For example, in 1984 Julia Kristeva published her *Revolution in Poetic Language* and in doing to proposed to the Anglo-Saxon feminism a way of looking at the world, and poetry, that was radically different from many of the more mechanical accounts of social reality in fiction offered by feminist critics. What Kristeva did in *Revolution in Poetic Language* was to propose that *avant-garde* writing in late nineteenth-century France (writing published at the point of the emergence of literary modernism) articulated what Kristeva described as the 'semiotic'. By this, she meant that the literature of the period was pre-symbolic – again, a reference to psycho-analytic (and particularly Lacanian) theories of language in which a distinction is made between the language of children before and after they enter the language mode of patriarchy. This form of language, based on strict and encoded rules of grammar and syntax is an essentially ordered world in which experience has to be organized within a formal structure of language. The 'semiotic' form of language, however, allows shifts, discrepancies and ambiguities in language that are not allowed in formal symbolic language.

What was – and is – exciting and radical about this thesis is that it appears to offer a way of interpreting changes in literary form between the nineteenth and the twentieth century. The conventional discussion of literature in the 1960s and 1970s argued (indeed it still does) that the novel – the archetypical and definitive literary form of bourgeois society – 'declined' in the twentieth century. Certainly, a consensus between all critics suggests that after about 1920 the self-confidence of narrative in the novel disappeared. To give examples: George Eliot and Tolstoy were replaced by Proust and Virginia Woolf. Now this shift was – before contemporary feminism and the 'new' criticism – largely regarded in negative terms, since male critics saw in the disappearance of narrative self-confidence something of a parallel with the disappearance of self-confident male heterosexuality. 'Modern' writing became equated with writing that reflected decadence and decline and a pre-occupation with subjectivity and introspection that had always been regarded with suspicion by conventional critics. Equally, what has to be observed (and this may have accounted for the wariness of male critics towards literary modernism) is an increasing toleration of 'endings' in fiction outside what Nancy Miller has described as the euphoric/dysphoric distinction. Miller's account of the narrative destiny of female characters in fiction suggests that their typical fate in the eighteenth and nineteenth centuries was either marriage and social integration or death/disaster and social alienation.[23]

This form of fictional resolution, together with the critical assumptions that went with it, were both challenged by feminist critics such as Kristeva. To Kristeva literary modernism was not to be equated with decline, but with the recognition of the diverse possibilities of the human condition – possibilities inherent in the initial, pre-Oedipal phase of the child before sexual identity (and with it a particular relationship to language) is finally resolved. It is the representation of the *lack* of resolution of the issue of sexual identity, and the continuity into adult life of what Freud called 'polymorphous perversity' that Kristeva and other critics found so engaging in late nineteenth-century literature. In opening up the possibility of the literary discussion of sexual ambiguity, Kristeva encouraged and inspired the work of Alice Jardine, Jacqueline Rose, Terry Castle, and many others on the multiple meanings of literature. In their readings and re-readings of literature, these critics suggested – and here Jardine was particularly influential – that modernism allowed women into discourse. In *Gynesis: Configurations of Woman and Modernity*, Jardine developed ideas suggested by Kristeva and proposed that although women were literally present (both as authors and as subjects) in eighteenth- and nineteenth-century literature, they were not present in any active, metaphorical or symbolic sense, since their very being was defined in terms of a fixed and rigid masculinity. When women attempted to negotiate their relationship to masculinity (and indeed their own femininity) then the story ended – as in *Madame Bovary* or *Anna Karenina* – in tragedy and tears. Thus what a conventional male critic such as Tony Tanner would see as a problem of adultery, and the literal form of sexual relationships, feminist critics began to read as a problem about the imposition on the imaginative world of fixed codes and practices of sexuality.[24]

Within this new reading of literature, Virginia Woolf very obviously assumed a central importance, since her work (whether fiction or non-fiction) is organized around the issue of identity and its fragility. In *Mrs Dalloway* (published in 1925) we can find a particularly vivid example of the way in which a woman experiences the apparently simple, everyday, experience of shopping in London. The private experiences and feelings of Mrs Dalloway are brought into a central place in Woolf's story, so that what is created is a thoroughly 'modern' account of urban life. The intense irritation expressed by a number of male critics at Woolf (both at the time and subsequently) then becomes part, and can be seen as, a continuing contest between women and men expressed in terms of fictional perceptions of the world. This idea – of the twentieth century as a battleground between the masculine and the feminine (although emphatically this is not always expressed in literal terms of the male and the female) has been developed by a number of feminist critics, amongst them Elaine Showalter, Sandra Gilbert, Susan Gubar and Ann Douglas.[25] All these writers have argued, with different emphasis, that the twentieth century has been an ongoing contest between 'feminine' accounts of experience (which have given space to subjectivity and allowed far from rigid distinctions between the public and the private) and those of the traditionally masculine, which have maintained rigid distinctions about narrative and the public and private. Nancy Armstrong, in *Desire and Domestic Fiction* (which was published in 1987) further proposed that the positive representation of conventional femininity was crucial to the very project of modern industrial society, in that by the construction of a humane, 'feminized', home the very form of bourgeois society could be interpreted, and defended, as positive.

Nancy Armstrong quite explicitly acknowledges her debt to Foucault, and in doing so is one of the many feminist critics who introduced into the literary criticism of the 1980s the idea that sex, and sexuality, are two different things. She writes, at the beginning of *Desire and Domestic Fiction*:

> [Foucault] asks us to think of modern desire as something that depends on language and particularly on writing. It is on this ground that his History of Sexuality assaults the tradition of thinking that sees modern sexuality as logically prior to its written representation.... According to Foucault, however, sex neither was nor is already there to be dealt with in one way or another by sexuality. Instead, its representation determines what one knows to be sex, the particular form sex assumes in one age as opposed to another, and the political interests these various forms may have served.[26]

In this discussion of Foucault, and the elaboration of his work that follows in *Desire and Domestic Fiction*, Nancy Armstrong goes some way to demonstrating that literature – and indeed any form of representation of human beings – is in itself formative, rather than simply mimetic. That is, that the putting into language of physical forms and human desires imposes upon them a certain kind of culturally formed identity. It is not that 'desire' is misrepresented, or that in its natural state it exists in some other form, but that we cannot escape from the limits (and indeed the possibilities) of the language that we have at our disposal. Thus the great enabling, and liberating, impact of Foucault's ideas is to suggest that representation does not in some sense 'uncover' or 'reveal' the 'truth' about human reality, but that it constructs versions of the 'truth' in different human situations and social contexts. What disappears with this argument is any set of ideas about 'normal' or 'real' sexuality: sexuality, according to Foucault, is all a construction and a changing construction at that.

Hence for feminist literary critics the possibilities allowed by Foucault become numerous. There no longer has to be a search for the literal woman, or female sexuality in the novel, because no such thing exists anyway. Similarly, in the cinema or photography or advertising or any other form that represents human beings, there is no necessary reason to accept literally the human forms offered. What disappears completely in this account of representation is any sense of art and literature as moral agents: the furore that has surrounded films such as *Pulp Fiction* is part of a post-modernist, and post-Foucault, context in which the body (whether male or female) is no longer encoded as morally and sexually fixed. This thesis has implications for the discussion of contentious areas of gender politics such as rape and pornography: on the one hand are those who argue a case that maintains the primacy and centrality of the literal, whilst on the other are those who suggest – for example – that rape only *is* rape because of the anachronistic importance that is attached to the male sexual organs. Put more simply: if we no longer construct the penis as a source of symbolic power, then we also de-construct its ability to inflict symbolic and/or physical and emotional harm. On that issue, not only is the jury still out, but the full cases on both sides still have to be put.

But what does now exist is a recognition that feminist theories of representation have to take on board an understanding not just of literal women, but of what Elizabeth Cowie has called 'woman as sign'.[27] A consensus does exist that women cannot be read (or represented) simply in literal terms, because in doing so we can too easily impose upon the represented female person highly subjective and often irrelevant judgements. It is, for example, too easy to read women in literature as victims, and – until recently – too difficult to read them as active subjects. Equally, it has often been too easy to read (or see) women as they are seen by men, and problematic to recognize the evasions and absences that are part of this representation. For example, one such absence is that of autonomous female sexual desire (whether for women or men) and the endless problems that this has created for writers and artists. It has long been recognized that the *explicit* discussion of sexual desire (whether of women for women, women for men, men for women or men for men) was a problem in the novel, and that most discussion was deeply coded, but *not absent*. What feminist critics have done, and most radically in terms of the discussion of sexual desire between women, is to argue that the imposition of rigid expectations of heterosexuality have distorted and/or misunderstood literature. Thus in *The Apparitional Lesbian* Terry Castle refers to what she calls the 'ghost' of sexual love between women and its presence as a central theme in fiction. Similarly in the context of sexual desire between men critics such as Eve Kosofsky Sedgwick have contributed to the naming and the understanding of homosexual desire in fiction.[28]

The numerous tensions and controversies that now exist within representation thus have to be seen in the context of the emergence, in the last twenty years, of feminist criticism and postmodernist accounts of representation. There is considerable over-lap between these two accounts of representation, of which the most important are the acceptance of the extensive boundaries of the subject (that is, the old distinctions between 'high' and 'low' art are no longer regarded as valid) and the sceptical regard for moral positioning in literary and artistic criticism. In this latter case there is certainly feminist dissent, in that arguments about pornography (in particular) have considerable heat to them.[29] Yet whilst controversy remains about the nature of the legitimate representation of women, what has shifted is the expectation that men should be in sole charge of the form of this representation. The 'male gaze', and its authority have effectively been de-constructed, and this work of de-construction has applied as much to visual as to literary representation.

If literature, and particularly 'high' Western literature, was the initial focus of feminist concern in the 1970s, it was very rapidly followed by a two-fold attack on the very *subject* of this critique. In the first place, black feminist critics (particularly in the United States) brought to the forefront of critical discussion the issue of race, ethnic identity and literature. In Anglo-Saxon terms the connections between the history of literature and the history of colonialism were unavoidable (Kipling, Forster and Conrad are just a few of the names who demonstrate the strength of this connection) but the critical literature on this subject was largely ungendered, in the sense of lacking an awareness of women *per se* and of non-white women in particular. But in the 1970s two strands developed within feminism that were to challenge this ethno-centric bias. First, what was hailed as a 'new' fiction by black women emerged in the United States. Toni Morrison, Alice Walker and Maya Angelou were amongst those whose work received widespread attention. With the emergence of the recognition of these authors came a re-discovery of the richness of black women's writing both in the past and in other cultures. The apparently 'new' was found to be a development rather than a radical innovation and in critical works such as Barbara Christian's *Black Women Novelists: The Development of a Tradition*, the distinguished and complex part of black women writers was given a voice. *Black Women Novelists* was first published in 1980 and as such represents an early part in the reclamation of black history. Since that time, further works have both enlarged the points of cultural reference and developed ideas about the 'boundaries' between cultures. As Maggie Humm has pointed out in *Border Traffic*, distinctions between 'black' and 'white' women's writing assume a rigid separation of cultures that may serve particular political purposes but are often far from the lived experience of social and cultural life.

Thus whilst the 1980s saw the emergence of a critique about the racial and ethnic identities obscured within ethnocentric perceptions of culture, what also emerged was an increasing scepticism about the distinction between 'high' and 'popular' culture. Feminism was hardly alone in attacking this distinction, since the development of cultural studies/media studies had already raised the academic profile of these areas. But what feminism did was to gender critical discussion in the area of what had once been described, dismissively, as 'popular' culture. As in other areas, second wave feminism evolved through a pattern of the literal recovery of women, followed by a re-evaluation of women in more symbolic and metaphorical terms.[30] In the mid-1970s the conventional feminist reading of women in cinema (or the visual arts in general) was that women were only constructed in terms of men; this was followed – in the 1980s – by work by feminist writers such as Jackie Stacey, Judith Williamson, and Annette Kuhn who demonstrated that the 'codes' of advertising (and the cinema) were far more subversive, and often transgressive, than generally supposed.[31] What was crucial to all these analyses, and what forms a central organizing thesis for feminist work in the 1990s on representation, is the growing acceptance of the idea of the complexity of meanings contained within a particular text or image, and the violence done to this complexity by external readings structured by dogmatic ideas or theories. An example of this understanding is Jacqueline Rose's exceptional study of Sylvia Plath, *The Haunting of Sylvia Plath*. In this study Rose demonstrates the dangers of imposing meanings on texts, and the vital importance of creating theoretical space for ambiguity and uncertainty. More than anything else, it is the achievement of feminist criticism to have demonstrated this case, and to have seized the space within post-modernist criticism generally, for a feminist presence.[32]

5
The Body

The previous chapter has emphasized the tremendous energy and creativity that feminist criticism – and indeed feminism – has introduced into theories of representation in the written and the visual arts. In this, feminist criticism has more or less universally sided with what we can describe as 'the modern', as opposed to 'the contemporary'. Essentially, what this implies is that in the interpretation of novels (or film, or photography etc.) feminists have been more inclined to see the text as unstable, and as an always imperfect account of social reality. Moreover, that very social reality that is being portrayed in literature or art is in itself full of contradictions, instabilities and incoherence. If there is a summary for 'the modern' it is that there is little that is fixed or absolute, and that it is the purpose of the arts to understand and to portray this resolute ambiguity. The social sciences and the humanities in the West have – in the last twenty-five years – seen an explosion of writing in what can be described as 'post-modernism' – that is the disappearance of the expectation of absolute and total explanations in any of the social or the humanities subjects.

But the relationship between feminism and post-modernity is a complex one, as was that between feminism and modernism.[1] The great British writer of modernity was, of course, Virginia Woolf, a woman who described with endless accuracy precisely the complexity of the individual subject that is seen as pivotal to 'modern' understanding. Woolf has, therefore, remained a central figure for feminist iconography, and indeed for anyone who is concerned with the study of the nature of 'being' in Western twentieth-century society. Yet what Woolf also managed to encompass in her prose was an understanding of gender and material difference: *A Room of One's Own* and *The Three Guineas* are definitive statements of the impact on women of sexual discrimination and – most clearly in *The Three Guineas* – the impact on the public world of the exclusion of women. Woolf definitely did not turn her back on what is known as the 'real' world, and throughout her life she retained a very sharp sense of the impact on women of being without money.

Thus Woolf, although writing in her fiction about the nature of subjective experience in twentieth-century urban society can also be seen very much in terms of those British feminist writers of the 1930s (amongst them Margery Spring-Rice and Margaret Llewellyn Davies) who campaigned around issues of women's poverty and exclusion from the public world.[2] The point of the example of Virginia Woolf in this context however, is to demonstrate that she represents the kind of 'split' that has always existed in feminism and feminist research, between those women who write and campaign around particular, empirical and by their very nature 'contemporary' issues, and those women who see such issues as inseparable from larger questions about the construction of the identity of women and the nature of femininity in the twentieth century. It is not, therefore, that feminism contains merely differences of interpretation about the world but that these interpretations derive, very often, from markedly different perceptions of the nature of contemporary society. The debates in the 1970s and the early 1980s over the issues of 'patriarchy' and the use of the word 'woman' were all part and parcel of this debate: the distinction between those intensely involved with the particular (equal pay, fertility control and so on) and those equally passionately concerned with the very diversity of experience and identity that seems to undermine an understanding of any given empirical situation.

The issue that perhaps more than anything represents this difference of understanding (and emphasis) is that of sexuality – 'body politics' as it became known in the 1970s. Hence this chapter is centrally concerned with the way in which feminism and women's studies has constructed, and re-constructed the body and the enormous range of debates that have taken place in the last thirty years around, quite literally, the *corpus* of human experience. In the beginning, the radical message of feminism was sexual libertarianism and the right of women to be sexually active within heterosexuality. This demand was part of the general sexual liberalism of the West in the 1960s; the climate was one of the ending of sexual taboos and questioning about sexual morality. The demands were also part of older traditions as well: long-established organizations in Britain and the United States had campaigned for the provision of contraception, the decriminalization of abortion and changes in the law about sexual behaviour. One thing is now immediately apparent to any feminist re-reading of this period of the making of sexual history: that it was organized and structured by an understanding of sexuality that emphatically named heterosexuality as 'normal' and equally emphatically demonized, and indeed marginalized in the case of male homosexuality, other forms of sexual practice. Thus throughout the later part of the nineteenth century, and certainly the first part of the twentieth century, the British State prosecuted, and often persecuted, male homosexuals. (That it did no such thing formally in the case of women was the result of the inherent, and ever-lasting, congenital failure of the British monarchy to imagine anything outside its own experience.)

As gay historians of both sexes have now documented, the law about male homosexuality was one thing and the toleration of homosexuality and homosexual life styles was quite another. Jeffrey Weeks, Sheila Jeffreys, Lillian Faderman and many other historians of sexuality have shown the degree to which the actual sexual histories, preferences and experiences of large numbers of people were constructed in ways entirely at odds with legal orthodoxy and social conformity.[3] The great hidden history of male bonding and male homosexual relationships is in the process of being written and made part of our general understanding of the past.[4] So too is the history of sexual relationships between women, relationships that were never, in Britain, formally illegal, but were often conducted with some wariness of conventional society. But what both histories add up to, and add to, is an understanding of our sexual past in which there was little that was 'conventional' or 'normal'. Indeed, the evidence now available suggests that 'normal' heterosexuality was as much a marginal experience as any other, and that its existence owes as much to individual fantasies about sexual law and order as it does to lived reality.

Yet when feminism first engaged with the question of sexuality in the early 1970s it did so largely, but not exclusively, within an understanding formed by the assumption of heterosexuality as 'normal' and – most crucially – within a discourse which emphasized sexual liberalization and emancipation. Even so, differences of approach and understanding were evident early in the 1970s, and examples in the work of two of the most famous feminist figures of the time exemplify this difference. The first instance is that of Germaine Greer, whose *The Female Eunuch* explicitly condoned female heterosexual activity, and whose other writings at the time were part and parcel of a permissive, libertarian discourse.[5] Greer wrote explicitly in favour of women's heterosexual practice: she challenged the double standard of sexual morality (which had always confined women to sexual passivity and absolute conformity) but essentially was an equalizer – that is, she wanted women's behaviour to come more into line with that of men. Her work attracted considerable media attention (then as now) and what she typified, besides the wish to bring women's behaviour closer into line with that of men, was a set of attitudes about 'permissiveness' in personal choice.

Nevertheless, Greer's sexuality was also rigidly located within heterosexuality, and the notoriety that she attracted was essentially that of the ancient attention directed towards women seen as sexually promiscuous, whether literally or theoretically. Kate Millett, on the other hand, found herself on the front cover of *Time* magazine and an international figure because, when challenged about her sexuality at a feminist meeting, she declared herself to be a lesbian. The challenge derived from the growing anger of women in the United States at the marginalization of lesbian women, and the identification of women's liberation with heterosexual libertarianism. Kate Millett, forced into public declaration about her sexual life, then spent the following decade writing about that sexual life, and about the agonies of the choice that was forced on her. As is apparent to any reader of *Sita* or *Flying*, 'coming out' for Kate Millett was neither easy nor straightforward. Nor did she find in her affairs with women any straightforward access to personal happiness and fulfilment.

But what Millett did do for her readers in her autobiographical works was to demonstrate that relations between women are not necessarily free of jealousy, bitterness, exploitation and betrayal. She was by far from the first woman writer to write of lesbian relations and love between women (there is a long tradition in the West of just such a literature) but her work was a crucial contribution to the emergence, in the 1970s, of what has become known as a 'lesbian consciousness' and a self-conscious examination of the reality of relations between women. In the early women's movement of the 1970s the tendency of many women's groups, publications and organizations had been towards the non-hierarchical, the sisterly and the whole-hearted endorsement of the feminine as benign and nurturant. This rhetoric was closely related to stated assumptions about the 'exploitation' and the 'oppression' of women, and the confident conceptual leap from the actual reality of the global evidence of woman's care – giving role to assumptions about individual women's caring capacities. *Flying*, and most particularly *Sita*, demonstrated that whatever the oppression and exploitation of women by men, the possibility of women's exploitation by women was very real.

Thus the two cases – Millett and Greer – suggest the diversity within feminism in the early 1970s and the many problems inherent in the construction of a feminist sexual politics. Lesbian women and heterosexual women both wished to validate their sexual practice, but for some time the nature of this validation remained deeply contentious. Most simply, the nature of the contention was the assertion, by lesbian women on both sides of the

Atlantic, that given the exploitation of women by men, any woman involved in a heterosexual relationship was 'sleeping with the enemy'. A pamphlet published in 1979 identified heterosexuality as the prime cause of the exploitation of women. The authors argued thus:

> The heterosexual couple is the basic unit of the political structure of male supremacy. In it each individual woman comes under the control of an individual man. It is more efficient by far than keeping women in ghettoes, camps or even sheds at the bottom of the garden. In the couple, love and sex are used to obscure the realities of oppression, to prevent women from 'identifying' their man as part of the enemy. Any woman who takes part in a heterosexual couple helps to shove up male supremacy by making its foundations stronger.[6]

The anger and passion of this language (and indeed the pamphlet as a whole) were part and parcel of a culture that emerged throughout the 1970s around the issue of sexuality and sexual practice. Just as male homosexuals expressed their fury at the absence of homosexual civil liberties (even after the 1967 Homosexual Law Reform Act in England discrimination against male homosexuals was manifest) so homosexual women increasingly expressed their rage at the heterosexual 'normality' within which they had to live. The endless Western assumption of heterosexual love and marriage, despite its manifest failures and its contribution to gender inequality and family instability, was a deeply oppressive normality for the many who dissented in practice (and in terms of sympathy) from its coercive implications.[7] Above all else, both groups fiercely dissociated themselves from the idea of the privileged status of heterosexuality.

The theoretical catalysts that empowered and enriched the feminist politics of sexuality in the 1970s and the 1980s were the work, it has to be said, of two men – Sigmund Freud and Michel Foucault. What they both did for feminist sexual politics was to shift the emphasis from a literal concern with the body to a range of ideas about the diversity of the body and the possibilities of sexual pleasure. Although the feminists writing in the early 1970s (and Millett and Greer were no exception) were largely opposed to Freud, his recovery – by Mitchell, Chodorow, Sayers et al. in the late 1970s – allowed feminists to develop ideas about sexual politics that did not depend upon the assumption of privileged male power.[8] At least as significant was the first English publication, in 1979 of the first volume of Foucault's *History of Sexuality*. The project was far from the first time that Foucault had written about sex, for in 1963 he had already suggested that:

> We readily believe that, in contemporary experience, sexuality has found once more a natural truth which supposedly waited for a long time in the shadows, under various disguises, before it had the right to come at last into the full light of language, and which only our positive perspicacity now allows us to decipher.[9]

That thesis – the critique of the idea that we are moving towards the understanding of 'real' sex – is a crucial element in Foucault, as is his assertion of the dismal Western prohibition of the discussion of sexual pleasure. In his biography of Foucault, David Macey summarizes Foucault's position thus:

> Foucault contrasts two primary discourses on sexuality: an *ars erotica* and a *scientia sexualis*. The former, assumed to exist or to have existed in China, Japan, India, Rome or Arab countries, represents an erotic art in which truth is extracted from 'pleasure itself', 'pleasure being understood as a practice and being recorded as an experience'. The West, in contrast, had developed a dismal *scientia sexualis* which, in order to tell the truth around sex, elaborated procedures organized essentially around forms of power-knowledge, as opposed to *ars erotica*'s rites of initiation. Its primary form of power-knowledge is the confessional mode which uses a criterion of truth that gradually migrates from its ecclesiastical origins to domains as diverse as education and psychiatry.... Sexuality is not some inchoate level of experience existing outside the discourse or dispositif of sexuality, but its product. In that sense, the only possible liberation is the liberation of pleasures from the regime of sexuality and sexual identities.[10]

Foucault is quoted at length here because his work was to have (and still has) such an enormous impact on all work on sexuality in the West, whether feminist or not. In his challenge to the belief in gradual emancipation towards some kind of sexual enlightenment he questioned one of the central beliefs of post-war Europe: that we are somehow moving out of a time of dark repression towards a new sexual Jerusalem of understanding and liberalism. Indeed, Foucault made possible the reversal of our taken-for-granted ideas about the Victorians by pointing out that only a society pre-occupied with sex, rather than absolutely refusing it, would seek to disguise the embodiment of the physical characteristics of the body. Always opposed to ideas about 'progress' and 'liberalization', what Foucault did was therefore to assert the need to abandon ideologies and rhetoric about 'good' and 'bad' sex.

The implications of these ideas for feminism were considerable. Feminist academics, like the great majority of Western academics of both sexes, had paid relatively little attention to the history or social relations of sexuality prior to Foucault, and so his work both opened up a new area of research and made radical suggestions about its theorization. It was too – and very much so in the case of feminism – a subject that was high on the agenda of academic feminism, since feminism of the 1970s gave, as we have seen, considerable attention to the politics of sexuality. Prior to the work of Foucault, what was known about sexuality, and sexual practice, was largely located within an empirical framework of gathering information; in the United States, Kinsey and his associates had established work on sexuality in the 1930s and various other individuals (for example Michael Schofield) had followed in the tradition.[11] But the theoretical impulse behind this work was to find out more about sexual practice; Kinsey, it is true, had used his work to challenge some of the milder expectations of heterosexual conventionality, but otherwise the work was seen as important largely because of its fact gathering properties. No work, it has to be said, had been done that was explicitly concerned with women or prepared to discuss the problems of asserting heterosexuality as absolute normality.

But the combined impact of Foucault's work and feminist politics rapidly shifted the established perimeters of debate and discussion. The women who challenged Kate Millett about her sexuality, and who were openly prepared to identify themselves as lesbians, were only one part of feminist politics about sexuality, but they were a very vocal and very important part. Their political voice, and their political impact, was such as to assert the importance of identifying women's experiences and women's sexual desires, rather than seeing women's sexuality as being constructed through a response to male sexuality. The politics associated with these ideas included women-only meetings, separation in all possible ways from 'male centred' institutions and ideas and the assertion of an absolute emotional difference between women and men. In feminist meetings throughout the West in the early 1970s, radical feminists, radical lesbians and radical feminist separatists gave voice with great urgency to the need to re-construct what Foucault described as the 'dominant discourses of sexuality'.

It soon became apparent that a crucial idea within any new politics of sexuality, or sexual politics, had to be the understanding of the term 'desire'. As women began to point out, a great deal of sexual practice in the West has been organized (at least in the nineteenth and twentieth centuries) around the idea of women as sexually passive and men as sexually active. The politics of sexual liberation had put this idea on the radical agenda of the late 1960s and early 1970s (and it is of course very much a theme of Greer's *The Female Eunuch* and Erica Jong's novel *Fear of Flying*) but the original re-thinking about the idea was largely structured in terms of maximizing women's response to men.

The turning point, or at any rate a crucial landmark in the history of feminist writing about sexuality, came in the mid-1970s with the publication of a number of academic papers by women about sexuality. The first of these was Mary McIntosh's 'Who Needs Prostitutes? The Ideology of Male Sexual Needs', that was published in a collection of essays edited by Carol Smart and Barry Smart. The paper (published in 1978, the same year as the same author's equally influential paper on 'The State and the Oppression of Women') argued that criminal justice policy (and policing) around the issue of prostitution is derived from the assumption that men's sexual desire is natural and implicit. Writing from within both a feminist and a gay rights perspective, the author suggested that this idea effectively made women passive 'receivers' of male sexual needs and completely ignored any social or personal factors that might exaggerate, distort or even merely structure male sexual behaviour. The assumption behind official thinking about male sexuality, Mary McIntosh continued, was that it had to be controlled, but that its essential form was inevitable and indeed natural.

The paper was enormously influential, since it challenged a whole range of existing ideas about the apparent natural order of sexuality: men (and boys) Mary McIntosh argued, were not necessarily of a single sexual character. The nature of masculinity – post 'Who Needs Prostitutes?' – was very much part of academic feminist concern, and has remained so ever since. At the same time, Mary McIntosh's emphasis on sexuality as *constructed*, and culturally structured, sat uneasily with radical feminist accounts of male sexuality which emphasized (and continued to emphasize) male sexuality as an essential and predatory force. It is worth noting, in this context, that Mary McIntosh's essay was published just one year after Susan Brownmiller's *Against Our Will*, an account of rape that had yet again proposed the natural sexual aggression of men towards women.

Yet at the same time as Brownmiller, and McIntosh, were setting out different feminist views on the social construction of male sexuality, others were beginning to explore the implications for women of ideologies that identified female sexuality as passive and to question received ideas about the absolute dominance of heterosexual discourse. In papers that were to be as influential as that of Mary McIntosh, Nancy Cott and Caroll Smith-Rosenberg turned to the nineteenth century to re-examine ideas about Victorian sexual codes and practices.[12] The article that appeared first (in 1975 by Caroll Smith-Rosenberg on 'The Female World of Love and Ritual: Relations between Women in Nineteenth Century America') also appeared as the first article in the first edition of *Signs*, the journal that was to become the leading feminist journal in the United States. This association is particularly interesting, and significant, in that it demonstrates the enormous progress that had been made in academic feminism by 1975 and at the same time exemplifies the tensions and contradictions that have always existed between academic feminism on the one hand and the women's movement on the other. The editors of *Signs* wrote in the first volume of the journal that:

> Scholarship about women is not new. They have long been subject
> to investigation. Some of it has been serious or sympathetic; some,
> trivial or hostile. What is novel is the amount of intellectual energy
> men and women are now spending on such scholarship and the
> consciousness that often frames their efforts.[13]

Two things are immediately noticeable about this statement of
intent: that women are 'they' to the all-female editors and that a
distinction is made between consciousness and intellectual
energy. What is suggested is that a generation of women are
motivated by feminist consciousness and are now able to give
that consciousness a credible intellectual form.

This endless tension between feminism and Women's Studies
(which is discussed in the next chapter) was, of course, present in
the articles – by McIntosh, Cott, Smith-Rosenberg and many others, who turned to examine the issue of sexuality in the 1970s.
Caroll Smith-Rosenberg's article, like that by Nancy Cott on
'Passionlessness' (which was published in 1978), turned to historical evidence to demonstrate the various ways in which women
constructed their own sexual and emotional lives and did so inde-
pendently of men. The conclusion of the article proposed that:
'the supposedly repressive and destructive Victorian sexual ethos
may have been more flexible and responsive to the needs of particular individuals than those of the mid-twentieth century.'[14]
This thesis – of a rich world of female emotional support and
contact – was to prove a crucial beginning to feminist histories of
sexuality, in that the material offered and the thesis proposed
(that sexual orientation is not organized as either homosexual or
heterosexual but falls into place along a continuum between
these two points) challenged the received wisdom of an absolute
domination of a single view of female sexuality. Smith-Rosenberg
(and other eminent North American feminist historians writing at
the same time, such as Linda Gordon in *Woman's Body,
Woman's Right*) did not reject the idea of conventional, and
socially powerful ideas. But what they did do was to challenge
the view that single ideas were absolutely dominant.

Yet at the same time as historians such as Gordon and

Smith-Rosenberg were pointing to the rich diversity of sexual and emotional patterns, others – and here Nancy Cott was crucial – were arguing that single ideologies about women were all-encompassing in the nineteenth, as much as the twentieth century, and that a great deal of social life was organized around a narrow set of expectations about the sexuality of women. Thus what Nancy Cott described as 'passionless' was in fact the rise of what she calls 'moral motherhood' as the appropriate mode of being for women in the nineteenth century. She writes:

> As the dominant feminine ideal of the nineteenth century, moral motherhood evolved in sharp contrast to the masculine ideal of individual worldly success.[15]

The thesis is an extraordinarily powerful one, and what it does is to suggest a new reading both of nineteenth- and twentieth-century literature and of social practices in the same centuries. Through Nancy Cott's thesis (which she illustrated very fully by reference to the eighteenth-century novel) we can see how the expression of women's autonomous sexual desire became impossible in the nineteenth century. For example, Mrs Gaskell's heroine *Ruth*, the mother of an illegitimate child, had to conceive that child in a semi-conscious state in order to appease the expectations of a Victorian reading public that did not countenance publicly active female heterosexuality. As is now very fully documented, nineteenth-century novelists (including Mrs Gaskell) did not *not* write about sex, but they were often forced to write about it in a deeply coded way that substituted such natural events as the weather for sexual expression.

At the same time as 'passionlessness' opened up new ways of reading literature, it also became a rich source of inspiration in terms of the investigation of the lived sexual experience of Victorian women and men. If it was the case that women could only expect to be 'good' if they were moral mothers then it occurred to many feminist historians that expectations and aspirations about sexually active and assertive women would have to be found in unconventional areas of the culture. And this, in fact, proved to be exactly the case: as white, middle-class women and men were locked into an emotionally paralysing embrace of the moral mother and the aggressive entrepreneur, so male sexual dissenters turned to women from other classes, and other races, for the deployment of their alternative sexual fantasies.[16] The construction of non-white women as dark goddesses of powerful sexuality became part of nineteenth-century British and North American sexual history, and with it the legacy of racist sexuality that still pervades both cultures, and often makes impossible Western understanding of the sexual codes of other cultures.[17]

Thus as a source of the inspiration of the further discussion of sexual codes and the construction of sexuality, 'passionlessness' proved a particularly fertile idea. Liz Stanley's account of the relationship between the Victorian servant woman Hannah Cullwick and her employer, and Rebecca Stott's essay on the 'dark continent' as a metaphor for Victorian sexual fantasy are just two examples of the way in which feminist writers developed the implications of the idea of the limits of Victorian femininity.[18] Equally important was the way in which an account such as Cott's enabled feminist historians to understand the motives and the forces behind the 'modernization' of sexuality that occurred at the beginning of the twentieth century. Just as Victorian sexuality (in all its complexity) became seen as 'traditional', so the sexual mores that were constructed at the beginning of the twentieth century became described as 'modern'.

But whilst the shift in sexual attitudes in the West at the end of the nineteenth and the beginning of the twentieth century was described as 'modern', the nature of the change was very far from uncontested, and in that contest can be seen some of the sharper conflicts that have informed not just the feminist but the general understanding of sexuality. In a sense, the controversy was (and is) about what sex is for: or, to put it another way, who decides the nature and the limits of sexual activity. The 'regulation of sexuality' as it became known on a hundred university courses throughout the West is a relatively uncontroversial idea (in that no-one disagreed with the idea that sexuality is regulated in all societies by a number of processes, both formal and informal) but what was more controversial is the question of who regulates what and for whom. Women – in all Western societies – had a long tradition of campaigning for access to contraception and abortion, but in the late 1970s and early 1980s that long-standing tradition, generally and previously associated with liberalization and modernization, came to be questioned.

The article that marked a watershed in feminist thinking about sexuality was Adrienne Rich's 'Compulsory Heterosexuality', which was first published (in *Signs*) in 1980. By the time the article appeared Rich was well known as an author and a poet, and as part of a lesbian tradition within feminism that had challenged (throughout the 1970s) the dominance of heterosexuality in discussions of sexuality. Rich's radical essay argued that:

> My organising impulse is the belief that it is not enough for feminist thought that specifically lesbian texts exist. Any theory or cultural/political creation that treats lesbian existence as a marginal or less 'natural' phenomenon, as mere 'sexual preference', or as the mirror image of either heterosexual or male homosexual relations, is profoundly weakened thereby, whatever its other contributions. Feminist theory can no longer afford merely to voice a toleration of 'lesbianism' as an 'alternative life-style', or make total allusion to lesbians.[19]

To demonstrate her case about the marginality (and indeed the invisibility) of lesbians and lesbian sexuality in mainstream feminism (both within and outside the academy) Rich took four texts by feminists published in the 1970s and argued that all of them – well regarded and widely reviewed within the feminist community – were largely ignorant of the discussion of lesbianism. The four texts were Barbara Ehrenreich and Deirdre English's *For Her Own Good: 150 Years of the Expert's Advice to Women* (published in 1978), Nancy Chodorow's *The Reproduction of Mothering* (published in 1978), Dorothy Dinnerstein's *The Mermaid and the Minotaur* (published in 1976) and Jean Baker Miller's *Towards a New Psychology of Women* (published in 1976). All these books emerged from the academy, all were written within the developing context of academic feminism in the United States and all – in Rich's analysis – ignored lesbianism and tacitly assumed heterosexuality to be the norm of female experience.

Rich's article made an immediate (and lasting) impact in the feminist community. She asserted that the very radicalism taken for granted by heterosexual feminists such as Chodorow et al. was in itself as oppressive and demeaning as the patriarchal assumptions that heterosexual women contested. The article, indeed, attacked the assumption that heterosexual women could ever be radical, given that by their very sexual choice they were identified with, and associated with, those individuals – that is, men – who carried what Rich saw as the deeply misogynist values of Western culture. Furthermore, what Rich also attacked was the political and social ground occupied by her target group, the ground being that of the white, middle-class United States. Other kinds of experience and understanding were as marginalized, she suggested, as that of lesbians. In particular, the argument continued, black women were wrongly perceived as victims within a heterosexual norm: Rich's thesis is that a lesbian reading of black women's culture shows a positive, and high degree, of woman-identified friendships and loyalties.

It is around this issue – of how relationships between individuals are perceived – that Rich's contribution was so important to feminist work. What she did was to show how culture and social personal relations might be re-read and re-interpreted in terms of putting relations between women and women before relations between women and men. From the first point of view it then became possible to see a social and personal dynamic that could be centrally concerned with maintaining women's relations with women (our mothers, daughters, sisters and friends) rather than with men. The considerable anthropological literature that demonstrates the centrality of women's ties with their children (rather than male partners) is part and parcel of this thesis; obviously, half of all children are male, but Rich's point (and that of other writers) is that the most enduring social tie is that which involves mother and child.

Since Adrienne Rich was well known as a poet and a writer (her famous essay on motherhood *Of Woman Born* was published in 1976 and had argued for the assertion of maternal power), 'Compulsory Heterosexuality' received wide attention, and fuelled the growing tradition within feminism – both academic and otherwise – that saw gender relations as an endless source of social conflict and, by implication, a source of cultural inspiration and innovation. In *Of Woman Born* Rich had distinguished between motherhood as a social institution and motherhood as experience. Her case was that the social institution constructed by men deprived women of their control and enjoyment of motherhood. Contrary to feminists such as de Beauvoir, Rich argued for the pleasure (both emotional and social) of motherhood and against the social structures that separated women from this potential source of power and pleasure.

But if an emphasis in Rich's own work was on motherhood, other feminist writers took from her writing the concern with constructions of sexuality as much as the issue of mothering. Writers such as Sheila Jeffreys developed a thesis about the history of sexuality that had a great deal in common with Rich's work and offered a powerful counter-argument to the interpretation of sexuality (dominated by the work of Foucault) that was influential in the 1980s. As suggested earlier in this chapter, what Foucault did was to argue that sexuality has been constructed – sex is constant, but sexuality is not. But for Foucault the politics of sexuality was always primarily about male homosexuality: his writing about female sexuality (whether lesbian or heterosexual) was limited and many of his arguments (such as his refusal of the meaning of heterosexual rape to women) has always enraged feminists. Thus Rich and Jeffreys emerged as a challenge to a view of sexual history and the sexual past that saw the oppression and persecution of male homosexuals as central and crucial: whilst Foucault saw the marginalization of gay men as the major sexual constraint of the twentieth century, feminist writers such as Rich and Jeffreys saw it as secondary to the demonization of lesbianism. A consensus emerged around the interpretation offered by Rich and Jeffreys: gay men might have been oppressed, but at least they were men and as such belonged to the sex that – in their view – effectively controlled the politics and culture of the West. Equally, when Foucault argued against the idea of a 'permissive' sexual culture, Sheila Jeffreys pointed out that Foucault's attack on the limits of permissiveness was about its limits for men; her thesis – fully developed in *Anticlimax* – is that the sexual 'revolution' of the 1960s was in actual fact nothing other than an extension of male rights over women, rather than anything approaching the genuine extension of sexual choice.

By the early 1980s it was apparent that within feminism, there was not just a diversity of views about sexuality, but hotly contested views. Many of these issues came to a head at a conference held at Barnard College, New York; indeed, the conference as a whole demonstrated the tensions that existed by that point between different views on feminism, feminist sexuality and the relationship between the women's movement and academic feminism. The context of the meeting was that of a series on 'The Scholar and the Feminist' that had been organized for nine years on the East Coast of the United States. The conference in question was to be on Sexuality. Reporting on the conference in *Feminist Review*, Elizabeth Wilson spoke of the tensions and antagonisms released and manifested at the conference; she wrote: 'events surrounding the conference have created consternation, anger and uproar amongst American feminists and deepened the already scarring divisions in the American movement.[20] In particular, furious debates took place around the issues of what 'feminist' sexuality is, the nature of pornography and the limits of the possible relationship between mainstream North American culture and feminism. The case was put (by Gayle Rubin and others) for the acceptance of sexual practices and sexual representation previously dismissed by feminism and the rejection of conventional values that constructed – as many participants saw it – a dominant heterosexual mode for women. Given that the conference series was funded by the Helena Rubinstein Foundation, it was little wonder that the dominant construction of American femininity should come under attack, nor that the nature of the relationship between the conventional world and the radical world should be raised.

In terms of feminist politics and theorizations of the body and of sexuality, the Barnard Conference marks something of a watershed in feminism. Prior to that date, it was clear that there was considerable diversity within the women's movement on the issue of sexuality: no-one reading the works published in the 1970s could doubt that. But the overall picture that emerged was that of white, heterosexual, middle-class women arguing for the re-organization of conventional discourses about the body and sexuality. The political issues that therefore received attention were those of greater flexibility about childcare and contraception: the issues that accompanied heterosexual sexuality. All feminists had subscribed to the assertion of lesbian rights and a lesbian presence, but on the whole this group of issues had been seen in terms of a sisterly culture of lesbian practice. At Barnard, and after it, the view of lesbianism as a gentler, more sisterly, form of sexuality was dismissed: what replaced it was the assertion of 'butch' sexuality and the acceptance of female sexual aggression directed towards women.

Throughout the 1980s the issue of what women should 'do' with their bodies remained politically explosive, yet at the same time writing on what is done to the female body (with or without female collusion and/or assistance) increased.[21] On both sides of the Atlantic, feminists demonstrated the de-humanizing practices of medicine on women in childbirth and the richly sexist assumptions that lay behind many models of medical intervention.[22] The body, female and male, and what is constructed from it, became a central issue in feminist thought. Equally, the body was scarcely over-looked in the mainstream, non-feminist, academy, and throughout the 1980s the body was, so to speak, at the heart of many academic debates. 'The body in question', 'bodies that matter' and 'gendering the body' all became widely familiar terms in the social sciences. By 1992 it was possible for Elizabeth Bronfen to write *Over Her Dead Body* and explore the aesthetic fascination of the dead (or dying) female body for Western writers and artists.

Thus by 1990 the body – and its perceived possibilities – had come a long way from the relatively static body proposed by feminists in the early 1970s. In those years, the two main theses had been either that women should be able to have more (and better) heterosexual sex on the same terms as men (à la Greer) or that women should have a different kind of sex, with women (à la Millett). Rosalind Coward, and others, effectively demonstrated the plurality of the idea of sexual 'desire' and thus – and together with the ideas of radical lesbians – came about the feminist re-writing of sexuality that was to characterize the 1970s and 1980s.[23] At the same time, it is crucial to remember that whilst feminism made great theoretical advances on the understanding of Western sexuality, conventional, mainstream practices and representations of sexuality remained deeply conservative. It became possible, on film and on the stage, to show more physically explicit sexuality (which generally meant female nudity and simulated heterosexual intercourse) but discussions and portrayals of heterosexual encounters remained paralyzed in a male predator/female seductress model. If women were sexually available, and sexually forward, in relations with men, then it inevitably followed that they were morally flawed: a version of female sexuality depicted by Hollywood in the 1980s that was as old as Western culture.

Into the debates within this discrepancy between the rigidly conventional mainstream and the increasingly radical sexual communities of feminism and gay men came, in 1990, Judith Butler's *Gender Trouble*, a book that received widespread attention for its rejection of given gender identities. To say that the book was not written for general audiences is something of an understatement for Judith Butler's argument rests heavily on an understanding of complex theoretical ideas. Essentially, what she sought to show was that although sex is discursively produced, 'gender is as determined and fixed as it was under the biology-is-destiny formulation.' Throughout the book, the notion of 'performative' gender is crucial to Butler's argument, and what can be discerned here – in terms of the relationship between mainstream and academic cultures – is a (deeply) theoretical account of the kind of androgyny made explicit in popular culture in the West in the 1980s. If Boy George stands as a symbol of that culture, then Judith Butler stands as its high theoretical priestess – a priestess who is concerned to show that what we assume to be 'natural' about our gender identity is almost non-existent, and should be made explicit. Thus Butler writes:

> The loss of gender norms would have the effect of proliferating gender configurations, de-stabilizing substantive identity, and depriving the naturalising narratives of compulsory heterosexuality of their central protagonists: 'man' and 'woman'.[25]

103

In effect, therefore, the thesis suggests not only the absolute instability of gender identity, but also the *merit* of this situation.

What Butler, and others, such as Elizabeth Grosz wish to do is to develop those ambiguities of gender made possible by intellectual and social changes in the West in the late twentieth century. For example, in the introduction to her study of Julia Kristeva, Luce Irigaray and Michelle Le Doeuff, Elizabeth Grosz emphasizes the possibilities given to feminism by Freud in his implicit critique of Western binary oppositions: once 'man' and 'woman' are de-stabilized, then it becomes possible to re-think the inherent meanings of gender.[26] Equally, Grosz, Butler and others recognize that reproduction is now possible in ways that subvert and indeed ignore conventional paternity: the 'new reproductive technology' makes possible new family relations. It is not that these new forms of reproduction have not been hotly contested (as the work of Corea, Duelli-Klein and Stanworth et al. has made clear) but the point is that they have provided a visible demonstration of the ways in which conventional gender expectations can be undermined.[27] Furthermore, a labour market that values skill and not strength and is increasingly organized in terms of part-time (not to mention low-paid) work is in many ways a further indication of the shifting social boundaries of the late twentieth century. But what Judith Butler's position would make possible – and hence its liberatory possibilities – is the disappearance of those fixed normative categories of 'man' and 'woman' that still exercise enormous ideological control over all aspects of our society. If we take the example of paid work we can still see the extent to which ideas about 'men' and 'masculinity' determine the location of professional and political power and with it the absence or the distortion of the feminine. Nevertheless, the *coincidence* of technological change and the weakening of the Western metaphysic of binary opposition suggests the possibility of new forms of gender relations that are not structured either by biological imperatives or the hierarchical dichotomy between male and female.[28]

Thus in the writing of Butler et al., we see the rich possibility of the re-construction of the body in terms that might allow both sexes to construct new forms of relationships (with themselves and with others) in which sexual difference is allowed but not given a hierarchical interpretation.[29] In reviewing the history of feminist writing on the body we can, therefore, see two major themes: one is to allow women to develop and to have an understanding of the possibilities of the female body that is not structured by male needs, and the other is to integrate an understanding of the body as a physical object with the body as a rich source of symbolic interpretation. Post-Freud it is impossible not to be aware of the 'psychical consequences of the anatomical differences between the sexes'; for feminists it is equally impossible, in the 1990s, not to be aware of the paradox of both the similarity and the difference of the female and male body. It is that paradox, which is also one of the dominating themes of the late twentieth century, that feminism has done much to explore. Yet at the same time, women live in a world that still maintains biological difference as social difference and that still asserts – particularly in cultures outside the West – a social and ideological separation of the sexes that underpins the continued economic exploitation of women.[30]

6

Feminism and the Academy

The preceding chapters will (hopefully) have suggested to readers that in the last twenty-five years feminism has introduced a new perspective into intellectual and academic life. A major part of that new perspective is the discussion of a gendered subject in the social sciences and the humanities: the recognition that the once universal 'he/man' of academic disciplines is only one half of the reality of human existence. The contribution of feminism has been to demonstrate that human society is made up of two sexes, and that the interaction between them (whether of consensus or conflict) is a major part of the dynamic of individual and social action.

But putting 'women' on to the contents list of the academy has only been one way in which feminism has challenged existing ideas and practices. That, in itself, is sufficiently radical to continue to provoke resistance and rejection, but where the idea has been accepted that women constitute half of the human subject, it has then become the case that the precise identity of those women becomes contentious. Who is the woman in the new academic area called Women's Studies? Thus the meaning of the category 'woman' becomes the subject of debate, a debate that in

106

turn raises complex issues about the meaning and function of the academy. If this was not a sufficient agenda, then it is also the case that Women's Studies has raised – from its very inception, issues about the power relations of the classroom and the academy and questioned the very ways in which 'knowledge' is constructed and assessed.

These issues, and this agenda, have made feminism an inherently de-stabilizing force in both intellectual life and the academy, even if at times the sheer strength of the academy to absorb and limit debate is more than able to limit the more critical and subversive elements of the subject. The feminism of the early 1970s, in which lie the political and intellectual roots of contemporary feminism, was unequivocally about disturbing and re-writing the Western order of relations between women and men. Anyone now re-reading the works by feminist authors of the early 1970s can have no doubt that the project of these works was both to re-think and to re-construct the social world in radically different ways: patriarchy was to be identified and overthrown and women were to assume a measure of hitherto unknown power and autonomy. The feminist projects that date from the early 1970s – of woman-run bookshops, health care centres and refuges for the female victims of male violence – were all the direct result of women's perception of the existing inequality in relations between men and women. Many of these projects still exist: the bookshops continue, the health care centres (particularly related to reproductive rights) still function and there has been a massive growth in the numbers of organizations and institutions dealing with crimes of violence against women. In all those cases, therefore, the impact of feminism has been considerable, and continues to demonstrate the vitality of feminist thinking.

At the same time, we have to observe that in the 1970s and 1980s there was a systematic erosion of some forms of female autonomy, as ideas about the 'progressive' nature of the ending of separate male/female spheres came into prominence. All-girls schools and women-only colleges in higher education were two obvious examples of this trend towards the abolition of the institutional separation of the sexes. In Britain, some hospitals attempted to introduce mixed sex wards and were amazed to discover that for most women and men this form of forced intimacy was wholly unacceptable. Thus did the general public – in just one example – resist what appeared to be a movement towards 'unisex' and androgyny. Whilst the superficial appearance of women and men may have become closer in the 1970s and 1980s (street style tending to obscure rather than exaggerate sexual difference) it was apparent that the confusion of style and fashion with behaviour and expectation was more than possible.

What is interesting about these issues of style and dress (so elegantly discussed in terms of their social implications by Elizabeth Wilson in *Adorned in Dreams*) is that in the 1970s and 1980s unisex dressing came to have what was in many ways conservative implications, and to be part of a general social resistance to the 'feminine' that has had, and continues to have, important implications for women. In the nineteenth and early twentieth centuries, it was socially radical for women, particularly white middle-class women to dress like men. For a woman to wear trousers was, as everyone knows, a highly subversive act and part and parcel of that vogue of the 'new woman' that was so generally attacked by conservative male critics at the end of the nineteenth century. For several subsequent decades, adopting male dress and behaviour (whether smoking or acting with a measure of social and personal autonomy) was part of women's resistance to conventional femininity.[1] But by the 1970s and 1980s to dress like a man, or to behave in accordance with 'male' standards about paid work or sexuality began to be more socially and politically problematic: the legitimate question could now be voiced about the limits of emancipation and genuine female liberation implicit in contemporary modes of appearance and behaviour. In popular mythology, for example films such as *Fatal Attraction*, the 'new' woman of the West was demonized as amoral and threatening to the male order of the universe.[2] At the same time, 'gender bending' allowed men – more so than women – to escape from the confines of traditional masculinity. In all these modes and spheres, the appearance of individuals came to carry deeply coded messages about sexual orientation, personal identity and political choice.

These disparate personal possibilities – all widely available to the majority of the population in any urban world – came to represent new perceptions of gender. Indeed, in many contexts the recognition of gender became associated with the traditional and conservative: the debates about mixed hospital wards were often conducted in terms of 'modern' attitudes and 'conservative' feelings of older patients. Thus, the very acknowledgement of different sexes became 'backward' and in some fundamental sense anti-modern. In exactly the same way the West has been able to launch its ideological attack on Islam in similar terms: the separation between the sexes in some Islamic countries is presented as primitive and incompatible with 'modern' life.[3] The Western way with gender, the argument frequently goes, is to assert that sexual difference no longer exists in any meaningful social sense: women and men are both citizens and – often more importantly – consumers in exactly the same sense. The manifest limitations of this view – that the labour market and the social world are deeply gendered – still has to be put to those whose conservatism blinds them to gendered social inequality.

These comments are made here to locate the meaning and the complexities of feminism more firmly within both general and academic contexts of the late twentieth centuries. Academics have all too often acted, and written, as if they exist on some separate planet from other people, and one of the many virtues of feminism was that it brought ordinary, everyday, reality into the academy. At the same time, those everyday realities were far from uncomplicated and thus what has become part of academic feminism is a recognition of the multiple – and often contradictory realities – within which individuals live and work. The second wave of feminism – in the 1970s – thus brought to the academy a determined sense of sexual difference, and the determination that the academy should recognize it. In this, feminism ran counter to the development of mainstream culture: just as the West was translating citizens into consumers (and with it passengers into customers and so on) what feminism has done is to assert the necessity of the recognition of sexual difference. It is little wonder then, that traditional misogyny and established academic interests scarcely welcome a form of critical inquiry that,

109

in addition to rejecting conventional assumptions, also challenges an important element in the development of what is perceived as 'modern'. Indeed, the argument can be made that feminism offers not just the academy, but contemporary Western thought a powerful antidote. In the face of a culture that appears to diminish sexual difference, yet is deeply fearful of female power, feminism offers the challenge of both asserting sexual difference and the right of women to personal and social autonomy. As Elizabeth Grosz has pointed out:

> 'Woman' represents a resistance, a locus of excess within logocentric/phallocentric texts, functioning as a point upon which the text turns upon itself.[4]

Moreover, she goes on to point out the important distinction made by Derrida about women and feminism:

> Derrida ... follows Nietzche's claim that there are two kinds of women: feminists, whose project is simply the reversal of phallocentrism, that is, who strive to be like men, to have a fixed identity, a natural essence and a place to occupy as subjects; and women who differ from rather than act as the opposites of the masculine, thus subverting and threatening to undermine masculine privilege. While clearly not mutually exclusive ... this distinction nevertheless involves a separation between those women who strive for identity (of whatever kind) and those who abandon the (phallocentric) demand for a stable identity, and de-stabilize logocentrism itself.[5]

But male culture, as feminists in many contexts have discovered, is often very complex and contradictory. Men do not share a common political position and the history of the world (as conventionally constructed) is a history of disputes between them. What they have seemed to share, at least as far as the academy is concerned, is a degree of resistance to the presence of women, whether literally or metaphorically. Thus the history of Western higher education is, in part, a history of the exclusion of women: not until the 1970s did women make up a significant proportion of the students in higher education in the West. In Western Europe and North America the proportion of female to male students is now everywhere equal, although what remains generally is a massive inequality in the numbers of female and male academics and senior university administrators.[6] The effects and implications of this have now been discussed by women academics; that the sex of the person teaching does have an impact on their teaching (in terms of both content and style) is the general consensus.[7]

So when feminists went into the academy, or became feminists within the academy, what we encountered was a world with a long tradition of the prioritization of male interests. That sense of priorities was both explicit, in the sense that the curriculum was demonstrably about men rather than women and implicit, in that the assumptions of male life, and a male career, were taken for granted. From the early 1970s, faced with the massive exclusion of women from the academy (as indeed was the case for other professions) women academics began to campaign around the essential issues of access to the professions for women: the issues of non-discriminatory appointments system, the recognition of the interrupted career patterns of women and the need for employers to re-think (or at least consider) their expectations about the relationship of individuals to their jobs. At the same time, women recognized that professional networking was essential, as was a visible and a collective presence. Thus women's networks developed both within universities and between women in different universities. Since one or two women, isolated in an all-male department or Faculty, could do little to challenge expectations or resist conventional pressures, the establishment of these networks was widely acknowledged to be of paramount importance.

Thus by the mid-1970s, women in the academy of the West could identify both general networks (in Women's Studies and other professional organizations) and networks in specific subjects, such as History and Sociology (for example, both the British and the American Sociological Associations had Women's Sections by this point). These networks were, and remain, supportive for women academics and allow some sense of the independence of women. What has gone with this development is also a sense of the inability of universities to shift easily the habits and assumptions of centuries. Throughout the West, there remains a general pattern of the resistance both to women academics *per se* and to feminist work. Although there is a considerable feminist presence in universities throughout the West, a general correlation exists between the degree of social exclusivity and privilege of a university and its limited toleration for anything approaching feminist work or Women's Studies. The case of the universities of Oxford and Cambridge provides a particularly telling example; both institutions have provided, in recent decades, plentiful evidence of discriminatory practice and a way of life – for both women staff and women students – that is deeply antagonistic and ingrained with what at times is simpleminded misogyny.[8]

The habits of behaviour and attitude of Oxbridge do not matter in any direct sense to a large number of people, but they clearly do matter in terms of academic authority and academic politics. The degree of control and influence of Oxbridge remains an important part of English academic life, and although other elite universities have successfully challenged the absolute intellectual authority of Oxbridge, it still remains the case that there is an *imprimatur* of authority about these institutions. In one sense, of course, the example of the absence of feminist pedagogy is another case instance of the conservatism of Oxbridge; both Oxford and Cambridge were equally slow to accept Sociology and the internal disagreements about the modernization of the Cambridge syllabus in English Literature received world wide coverage and discussion.[9]

Yet the debates within the Cambridge English Faculty serve to illustrate the telling point about the fierce resistance of the powerful to views of the world that challenge their own. The academy throughout the West prides itself on the idea of objectivity and the pursuit of truth. The *absolute* credibility of this view, in practice, has long been challenged and recognized as impossible. Throughout the twentieth century, a series of writers – many of them very distinguished academics themselves – have pointed out that universities have frequently acted as functionaries for the rich, the powerful and the corrupt. Robert Lynd's *Knowledge for What?* and C.W. Mills' essays on the links between universities in the United States and the interests of the American military provided cornerstones for a tradition that was subsequently developed by Noam Chomsky and E.P. Thompson in the 1970s.[10] Both these men, writing at the time of the emergence of academic feminism, stressed what they saw as the destruction of the independence of the academy by directly political interests. In the case of Chomsky's arguments, his case revolved around the massive contracts for military research (or research related to military interests) at universities in North America, and in particular the one at which he worked, the Massachusetts Institute of Technology. Thompson's case, about the funding of Warwick University and the university's apparent receptivity to the interests of the local business community, was equally passionate: that universities were effectively being 'bought' by outside interests.

The case made by E.P. Thompson in *Warwick University Ltd* now appears even more timely. The qualification that has to be made, however, is that whilst Thompson was dealing with absolutely explicit invasions of the university by commercial interests, what has occurred since the book was published is a more subtle and less explicit intrusion into the academy of managerial ideology. This point is made here to emphasize that universities themselves are complex institutions, both in organizational and ideological terms. Thus to see universities, and the academy generally, as 'male' detracts from, and obscures, other important issues about the universities in the late twentieth century. For example, in the case of Britain, the universities have been under pressure to increase the number of students and to do so without additional resources in terms of academic staff. The particular consequences for women of this change are, as ever, double-edged: on the one hand, there is no doubt that increased access to the system has given more women the opportunity of higher education. Thus in Britain – and indeed throughout much of the West – there are now equal (or nearly equal) numbers of women as men undergraduates, with a pre-dominance of women in the social sciences and humanities. On the other hand, there has been little change in the number of women academics and the widespread casualization of the system has meant that very often

113

where women are appointed, they are appointed to inadequately tenured positions.

Hence it is now the case that throughout the West women represent about half the student intake to higher education, without any corresponding shift in the number of women academics or senior administrators. Whilst reform of the recruitment practices into the academy (and its mode of working) would seem to be long overdue, so too is reform of the curriculum. It is here that feminism – in the form of either Feminist Studies or Women's Studies – appears in the academic space. We have already seen that the original links between second wave feminism and the universities were very close. Indeed, it was an admirable part of the culture of universities in the West in the late 1960s that universities were so engaged with politics and day-to-day questions of social life. (The managerial style in contemporary universities – particularly Britain – has served particularly badly those interested in the discussion and production of ideas rather than the processing of graduates.) Inevitably, given those close links between feminism and universities, women began to ask for a re-examination of what they were required to teach, if academics, and be taught, if students. Thus there was a heady proliferation of courses and degrees: by 1980 there were courses, if not degrees, about women at the majority of universities in Britain, the United States, Canada, Australia, Holland and Scandinavia. Other countries, for example in Europe the countries of the Mediterranean, were slower to follow suit, but in some instances this was due as much to the limitations of authoritarian and archaic university systems as resistance to Women's Studies *per se*. Generally, however, the pattern was one in which the countries of 'the North' could demonstrate an increasingly visible academic presence for women.

But with this new presence came a number of problems. In the first place, it was generally the case that Women's Studies in the universities had to fight endless academic battles about recognition and funding. Like any new subject, this one was resisted, and often marked out for special ridicule because its subject matter appeared limited. (Counter-arguments, about the traditional academy representing nothing except Men's Studies flew around throughout the 1970s and 1980s). Only gradually did senior male academics begin to realize that given the changed nature of the student population, Women's Studies might well constitute a more than viable subject. Thus one of the ironies of the history of Women's Studies in Britain in the 1980s was the increased toleration for it precisely because of market factors, and the income potential for Women's Studies.

Aside from those institutional issues of resistance and refusal, Women's Studies also faced a more complex form of rejection because of its manifest assertion of sexual difference. Entrenched interests were at stake in the academy – and always will be – as subjects competed for funds in an increasingly under-funded sector. But more than that, Women's Studies' mere presence was (and is) an endless reminder to male academics that their construction of knowledge has been partial and limited. Male academics have fought to include the male working class and non-white people in the syllabus; including women has everywhere been yet another frontier that has more or less exclusively been fought by women. Men, Freud observed (and here we should endorse the use of the sex-specific term) did not take kindly to having their 'naive self-love' disturbed by Copernicus's discovery that their earth is not the centre of the universe, nor to Darwin's demonstration that their species was not the first. Most importantly, Freud suggested, men do not like to be reminded (as he put it) that 'the ego is not even master in its own house'.[11] Thus the inherently assertive nature of Women's Studies, with its absolutely clear statement of intent, is an implicitly disruptive idea for many male academics: having staked all on the universal legitimacy and validity of a particular version of rationality, it is deeply galling to have this vision of the world challenged.

Thus it is possible to say, without risk of over-generalization, that all universities in the West extended a rather less than enthusiastic welcome to Women's Studies. The degree of coldness varied from place to place, and changed throughout the 1980s, but the overwhelming impression given by universities was that Women's Studies was less than welcome. At a time when (and certainly in Britain and the United States) the university curriculum was extending to include more and more explicitly vocational subjects, and research geared directly to the interests of the capitalist state, it was all the more striking – although hardly surprising – that a potentially critical voice within the curriculum was largely marginalized. But it would also be far from accurate to suggest that all opposition to Women's Studies came from male academics concerned about the disruption of the traditional syllabus. Opposition also came from both men and women academics on the academic grounds of concern for the integrity of the conventional academic discipline and – even more vociferously – from women outside the academy who saw in Women's Studies the dilution and the disappearance of the energies and the vitality of the women's movement into the black hole of the academy. With some reason, considerable concern was voiced about the viability of Women's Studies in maintaining anything like a radical, let alone comprehensible, view of the world once it entered the portals of the academy.[12]

Thus women academics who wished to introduce Women's Studies into the curriculum, and to suggest new ways of teaching and doing academic research, often found themselves attacked from many sides. Traditionalists argued that Women's Studies was a subject without an intellectual base, without, indeed, that most sacred of academic histories, a theoretical tradition. Critics of Women's Studies would point to disciplines such as Sociology and English Literature and lavish praise on their 'great tradition' and 'founding fathers', without hesitating to point out that such traditions were themselves both relatively recent and hotly contested. Indeed, to speak of 'a' theoretical tradition in most disciplines in the humanities and the social sciences was a nonsense, since all had long histories of diverse theoretical traditions and contested central themes. Nevertheless, whatever the rights and wrongs of their intellectual authority, it was still the case that traditional subjects occupied entrenched academic space: traditional subjects had university departments and university appointments organized around them and breaking into, and through, this stranglehold on resources and academic legitimacy has proved a long and difficult battle for Women's Studies.

Yet at the same time as Women's Studies has had to battle for academic resources in a political and economic climate that has everywhere seen the decrease in spending in higher education, it has also benefited – and paradoxically so – by the increased pluralism within the academy and intellectual life. In large part, this has been due to the acknowledgement, throughout the Western academy, of post-modernism and its intrinsic diversity of subject and perception. Thus in the early days of Women's Studies – the 1970s – the authority of conventional subjects was absolute. Increasingly, throughout the 1980s, that authority was systematically dissolved as theoretical pluralism was acknowledged. Hence a curious situation has developed throughout the Western academy, in which there is more inter-disciplinary, and cross-disciplinary academic work than ever before and the exciting work in all subjects is often taking place at the limits, rather than centres, of disciplines. Equally, those students who are not taking explicitly vocational degrees are putting together degree packages of diverse subjects. In this intellectual climate, Women's Studies can clearly flourish, and indeed has done, as the considerable volume of work produced suggests. At the same time, intellectual productivity has had to take place in institutional frameworks that still favour the 'traditional' disciplines, and implicitly discriminate against more innovative, cross-disciplinary work. The discrimination – very much in terms of the key resources of jobs and research support – continues at the same time as the continuing intellectual vitality of Women's Studies.

As is hopefully apparent from the above, Western universities are not the same place in the 1990s as in the 1970s, and this point is emphasized to locate Women's Studies within a particular context, and, preserve it from that sense of separation from the real world that is too often the case for academic concerns. The universities that resisted Women's Studies in the 1970s were universities flush with state resources, and at the height of a wave of the establishment of new posts and new courses. Paradoxically, the universities that tolerate Women's Studies in the 1990s are largely under-funded institutions that are attempting to implement public expectations of mass higher education with little additional funding. In the concern over funding, which everywhere dominates university agendas, concern over *what* is

117

taught is rather less crucial. Hence the new freedom is one produced by a context of material constraint and limitation.

Within this context, Women's Studies has generally flourished in the West, and in Western universities. The United States, Australia, Canada, Great Britain and the Netherlands are countries where the institutional presence of Women's Studies in higher education is universally apparent, if often limited and marginal. The suspicions about the loss of energy from the women's movement to academic feminism are still voiced, but that comment is now itself part of a tradition and a community that can point to the successful integration of ideas developed and systematized in the academy with a wider social world. At the same time, the change in the very nature of higher education, from elite to mass system, has made it difficult to make the same case about the distinction between the privileges of the academy and the rest of the world. Indeed, feminists (both within and outside the academy) can point to the influence of feminist academics such as Jalna Hanmer, Catherine Mackinnon and Ann Oakley. In the case of the issues of violence against women, pornography and the law and the medicalization of childbirth, all have made an impact far beyond that of the lecture hall or the seminar room.[13] As suggested, what has been partly responsible for the growing acceptance by feminists of Women's Studies is the recognition that the universities are no longer servicing a small elite, but a considerable part of every generation. Nor is it generally still assumed that universities are 'separate' from the rest of the world: the impact of Thatcherism and the market economy has created a situation where many academics might well wish for a return to the ivory tower, as a defence against the intrusion of market-dominated ideas into all areas of university activity.

Thus in the 1990s, many of the arguments about the degree of separation and difference between the university and the rest of the world have lost their credibility, and it has been widely recognized that struggle for the acceptance of feminist ideas is just as much possible within the academy as outside. The idea of the academy as a *site of struggle* was developed in the 1970s, and has remained as crucially significant. But at the same time as the engagement of the academy and the rest of the world has been recognized, equally influential has been the import into the academy of ideas about power relations and the social construction of knowledge. Within Women's Studies feminist academics have done a good deal to raise crucial questions about the relationship between the teacher and the taught, the observer and the observed. Again, raising these issues was not the sole responsibility of Women's Studies, since critical voices in other disciplines had long asked questions about the relations between researcher and researched, but for feminists it became an issue of particular importance. Liz Stanley and Sue Wise, for example, in their innovative writing on the subject suggested that a major responsibility of the researcher was to recognize their *own* values and their *own* position. They argued:

> Truth is a social construct, in the same way that objectivity is; and both are constructed out of experiences which are, for all practical purposes, the same as 'lies' and 'subjectivity'. And so we see all research as 'fiction' in the sense that it views and so constructs 'reality' through the eyes of one person.[14]

What was liberatory about these remarks (published in 1983) is that they, in effect, allowed the researcher the freedom both to interpret other people's behaviour and values and to involve, and to include explicitly, their own. What was being abandoned here was the figure and the person of the social scientist as the non-human, or at least a-social, seeker after truth. Stanley and Wise proposed, in fact, something that many people had long suspected about works of ethnography or social observation: that truth lay in the eye of the beholder quite as much as in the reported 'facts' of any given situation. The implications of this position were, and are, breath-taking: it suggests that an immediate re-evaluation is essential for virtually all works of ethnography, social investigation and, indeed, of the discussion of individuals and individual works. By the late 1980s this powerful scepticism about the 'truth' (and absence of it) of all reported social observation had led to the publication of studies such as Katy Gardner's *On the Water's Edge* that offered a reading of a society and a set of social relations in which the author's

119

difference from that society and culture was part of the narrative. Compared to the 'classic' texts of British anthropology, in which the viewpoint of the white male is never problematized, *At the Water's Edge* suggests the degree of intellectual shift that has occurred in the last twenty or thirty years: the author is now an active presence in the text and very far from the shadowy, or absent, person beloved of previous generations.

Thus ideas such as those of Wise and Stanley could be – and were – taken and developed in numerous subjects and diverse contexts. Women recognized that they did not necessarily need permission in order to state their views, or establish their agency. That stultifying sense of fear about the status of the academic audience began to diminish as the nature of the audience changed: no longer were women writing and publishing for men, they were now writing and publishing for themselves and for an audience that recognized as legitimate the status of the first person singular. Clearly, this new sense of freedom was likely to be rapidly apparent in those disciplines where the claims to objectivity were highest, and thus it was in sociology, psychology and social anthropology where a generation of women made themselves, quite literally, visible. Throughout the 1970s and the 1980s it became commonplace for academic authors to describe themselves, and situate themselves, as well as the subjects of their research. With this approach, in which the identity of the author was made explicit, came the assertion of the legitimacy of the autobiographical and the biographical as relevant academic material.[15] The person, and the individual, very rapidly came to acquire a new status as women academics everywhere asserted the importance of the human subject. With this shift came too a re-evaluation of classic texts, re-read and re-interpreted in order to demonstrate the partial gaze, and indeed the excluding gaze, of the quasi-objective method. Freud's account of Dora was just one such text to receive considerable scrutiny: a series of feminist scholars pointed out that what Freud did not include in his discussion of Dora's supposed pathology was any understanding of Dora's attempt to resist patriarchal influences and pressures. The key idea of the *absences* and the *evasions* in any text can be seen by these accounts of Dora; all the authors wish to demonstrate that the one thing Freud could not acknowledge was his own bias towards the interests of conventional patriarchal society.[16]

There are now numerous other examples of the ways in which feminist academics have re-read and re-interpreted the canonical works of Western civilization. This kind of re-reading has had a radical and radicalizing impact throughout *and beyond* the academy, in that since the intervention of feminist perspectives no classic work of the West (be it fiction or otherwise) can be read in quite the same, un-gendered way. Thus feminism, in its academic form, has to a large extent de-stabilized the Western canonical tradition and contributed, in a very important way, to the idea that no text is stable.[17] Much of the theoretical inspiration for these ideas has come from male writers (Derrida and Lacan are two particularly important presences in feminist writing) but the development and the integration of the ideas with existing traditions has been specifically feminist, in that women have been primarily concerned to demonstrate – through the use of particular theoretical innovations – the blindness of patriarchal knowledge to the experiences and aspirations of women. This position, with its manifest implications for the re-interpretation of all academic knowledge, has come to be theorized as 'standpoint theory' – the assertion, in fact, that the position and the person of the researcher are crucial ingredients in the outcome of the research process. As Sandra Harding has suggested:

> Once we undertake to use women's experience as a resource to generate scientific problems, hypotheses, and evidence, to design research for women, and to place the researcher in the same critical plane as the research subject, traditional epistemological assumptions can no longer be made. These agendas have led feminist social scientists to ask questions about who can be a knower (only men?); what tests beliefs must pass in order to be legitimated as knowledge (only tests against men's experiences and observations?); what kinds of things can be known (can 'subjective truths', ones that only women – or only some women – tend to arrive at, count as knowledge?); the nature of objectivity (does it require 'point-of-viewlessness'?); the appropriate relationship between the researcher and her/his research subjects (must the researcher be disinterested, dispassionate, and socially invisible to the subject?);

121

what should be the purposes of the pursuit of knowledge (to produce information *for* men?).[18]

It is thus the case that in the mid-1990s feminism can claim to have developed one of the now great critical traditions within the Western academy, that of suggesting that the universalistic assumptions of knowledge in our society are false, and partial, because they are drawn from the experiences of only one sex. Men's dominance of the public world, possible because of their relative absence from the private world of the household, has allowed them an unequal share in the construction of the discourses that dominate both public and private worlds. It is not that these discourses have not been both shared and contested by women, but it is that powerful men have confused *their* experience with *all* experience. The difference, as women (and people from minority groups) have pointed out, is considerable. ('The individual subject', as Catherine Hall has pointed out, 'was central to political thought and action, but that individuality was based upon difference and on "others" '.)[19] The re-making of the academy, to allow diversity and difference, is thus a major terrain of feminism. A large canvas, but one which offers some possibility of producing a knowledge of the world that is derived from a shared experience of it.

7

Worlds of Difference?

The concluding sentence of the previous chapter suggests that feminism, and feminist knowledge, offer rich possibilities for the re-thinking and re-ordering of our analysis and understanding of the social and intellectual world. It is an optimistic note, and one that perhaps demands further elaboration given the frequent assertions that feminism is dead or that it belongs only to some kind of pre-modern past, which is long gone.[1] The material referred to in previous chapters points to the very different social experiences and expectations of women and men. In the face of the contemporary rebuttals of feminism it is important to re-state, and re-assert, the relevance of that literature. Yet, at this point, it is also the moment to return to the assertion in the introduction that the worlds (and knowledge) of women and men are not so much separate as inter-woven, but inter-woven in a social context that allows the domination of male interests. Hence the importance of an exercise in unpicking the particular from the universal; without that assertion of difference there is little that can be changed about our understanding and practice.

Much of the material that has been collected by feminists in the last twenty years has been concerned, for very good political reasons, with the documentation of the marginalization or the suppression of women's interests and female identity. It has been, and it remains, essential to assert that in many crucial instances women do not share the same experiences as men or have the same needs or interests. As suggested in previous chapters, without campaigns organized around the concept of sexual difference, changes in the law on sexual violence might not have been made. Yet what remains an open question is the point at which differences of gender become insignificant, or at least less significant than differences in class, race and ethnic identity. In recent years two aspects of the limits of general assumptions about women have brought out the complexities of this issue. The first is the case of the continuing tragedy of the war in the former Yugoslavia. In that war, women, as victims of systematic rape, have clearly been 'read' and treated as legitimate targets of male sexual desire. The degree, circumstances and extent of these assaults remains unknown, but what is apparent here is that individual female human beings have been allowed no negotiation or discussion in the interpretation by men of their gender. 'Performing sexuality' was not an option in these cases, nor were other theories about the ways in which both sexes are imprisoned within conventional and circumscribed models of desire. Whilst people living short distances away from Bosnia were able to continue to debate the shortcomings (or otherwise) of contemporary theories of gender, an ancient form of gendered brutality was acted out by close neighbours.

The paradox (or part of the paradox) of the horrors of the war in Bosnia was that within the former Yugoslavia there had been both a determined peace movement (immediately marginalized by conventional politics both inside and outside the country after the outbreak of war) in which many women were active and an official political culture that largely denied the elaboration of 'bourgeois' forms of sexual difference. Thus the society had been rich in tensions between the independent activity of women and the prescriptive attitudes of the state to the public demonstration of conventional femininity. In this, of course, Yugoslavia had fallen into the general pattern of state socialist societies of attempting to minimize gender differences, and most visibly in the form of dress and appearance. When President Kennedy met Nikita Khrushchev in Vienna in 1961, one of the vivid visual messages of that meeting was the contrast between their wives; the difference in appearance between Jacqueline Kennedy and Mrs Khrushchev remains, to this day, a vivid personification of the assumptions of the West and state socialism about appropriate femininity.

But that contrast, between the slim elegance of Jacqueline Kennedy and the solid outline of Mrs Khrushchev (and readers will note that she remains firmly located within the label of her marital status), should remind us that we need to ask questions about the societies in which we, as women, live. The Western assumption of the individual is, as Catherine Hall so pertinently remarked, one constructed through difference and separation from others. As women we come to learn the limits of this belief, yet at the same time we are often loathe to recognize the ways in which we are creatures of our circumstances. Thus whilst an immediate response to the appearance of Jacqueline Kennedy might be, or might have been, one of envy and admiration, what feminism has taught us is that women's appearance, indeed our very identity, is constructed for a male gaze and may be far from expressing any real independence or autonomy. Again, the argument is complicated by a perception – derived from Western feminism – that the appearance of women is often closely related to the power and status of their male partners. Jacqueline Kennedy was not, therefore, Jacqueline Kennedy so much as she was the wife of the president of the richest society on earth. To a feminist brought up under communism this difference in style involves an understanding of different forms of social relations. Writing in 1992 Slavenka Drakulic commented on Eastern Europe:

> Walking the streets of Eastern European cities, one can easily see that the women there look tired and older than they really are. They are poorly dressed, overweight and flabby. Only the very young are slim and beautiful, with the healthy look and grace that go with youth. For me, they are the most beautiful in the world because I know what is behind the serious, worried faces, the unattended hair, the unmanicured nails; behind a pale pink lipstick that doesn't exactly go with the colour of their eyes, or hair, or dress;

125

behind the bad teeth, the crumpled coats, the smell of their sweat in a streetcar. Their beauty should not be compared with the beauty that comes from the 'otherness'. Their image, fashion, and make-up should be judged by some different criteria, with knowledge of the context, and, therefore, with appreciation. They deserve more respect than they get, simply because just being a woman – not to mention a beauty – is a constant battle against the way the whole system works. When in May last year an acquaintance of mine, a Frenchwoman, visited Romania (while there was still street fighting in Bucharest) she told me this about Romanian women: 'Oh they're so badly dressed, they don't have any style at all.' Beauty is in the eye of the beholder.[2]

To look at Mrs Khrushchev from this point of view allows us, therefore, to see past the apparent difference between that woman and a Western icon and observe real differences in relationships to the world, to sexuality and to the gaze of significant others. But to do this demands conscious and explicit effort, since what Western culture has achieved in the twentieth century is an astonishing acceptance on the part of other cultures of its values and its aspirations, not least in terms of appearance. Monroe, and Jacqueline Kennedy, became the globally known images of this culture in the 1960s, just as in later decades younger women (such as Kate Moss and Madonna) received similar acclaim. To be young, to be slim, to be Western (or Westernized) was the implicit goal set for women by these images: images that were reinforced by statements such as that by a former President of the United States, George Bush, that the American way of life was 'not negotiable'. Whatever the costs (both inside and outside the United States) it was made absolutely clear by this remark that the most powerful society in the contemporary world did not intend to alter its assumptions about consumption and the global distribution of resources.

Three years after this remark was made, the 'World Forum on Women' in Beijing in 1995 demonstrated the uneasy, and intensely problematic, relationship between women and contemporary politics. What came together at that meeting were demands for the sexual emancipation and autonomy of women – the acceptable face of modern capitalism – with demands for women's fuller participation in the workplace that entirely took for granted the global acceptance of capitalism. This meeting, descriptions of which could fill many pages, once again demonstrated the complexity of women's relationship to the public world and the strengths and limitations of the idea of unity between women. Women at Beijing representing nations of the South re-iterated the nature of the problems facing women in their countries: problems of the absence of clean water, primary health care and minimal education. Women from countries of the North could empathize with these demands and needs, whilst having to face the reality of a distribution of global resources that endlessly prioritizes the interests of the North (and its living standards) over those of the South. Inevitably, the presence of Hillary Clinton, the wife of the President of the United States as the 'keynote' speaker only reinforced the assumption that it would be from the West that definitive statements on the position of women would come. The model of womanhood that Hillary Clinton presented was very different from that of Jacqueline Kennedy, but it was still one which emphasized the values of the Western model of female emancipation, autonomy and achievement being central to that model. The distance between the appearance of Hillary Clinton and the reality of the lives of most of the world's women was a point not lost on many of the delegates.

Yet in pointing to this distance, and this difference, what we can also point to are the questions raised by it about who sets, and who decides, women's agenda and the degree to which women wish to participate in exactly the same way as men in the structures of the market economy. The shift between Jacqueline Kennedy and Hillary Clinton is important here, because in it we can see the shift, at the end of the twentieth century, of Western women into the public world and the grudging acceptance of women in that sphere. What Jacqueline Kennedy personified (at least when married to John Kennedy) was the beautiful goddess of the private sphere: the immensely powerful public man would – and could – produce from the private world of the household a person who demonstrated the values of that culture about female beauty. We now know that the Kennedy private world was no less fraught than that of the public world of politics. But what was also accepted, at that time, was a separation between the public and the private that largely excluded women from the public world and maintained secrecy about the private behaviour of the powerful. By the time Bill Clinton became President of the United States, the boundaries between the public and private had shifted: Clinton's sexual history was discussed in a way that was never true for Kennedy and his marriage to a woman who was demonstrably successful in the public world was regarded as both a positive asset and an indication of Clinton's modernity. Thus by the end of the twentieth century what was held up for admiration and emulation in heterosexual relations was a relationship in which both partners had apparently the same access to the public world and could play an equal part in the negotiation of the marriage contract.

The word 'apparently' is used advisedly, since what became transparently clear after Clinton's inauguration was the limited degree of toleration that actually existed for Hillary Clinton's intervention and participation in the public sphere. 'Staying home and baking cookies' began to look like a politically viable option as conventional expectations of female behaviour began to make clear the limitations of 'modernized' heterosexuality. Throughout the West we can see that despite rising divorce rates and a transformation in social expectations (and indeed experiences) of family and personal life there are still important divisions and distinctions between the ways in which women and men can participate in public life. The possible range of discourses about female and male behaviour has been extended (Western culture can tolerate and indeed endorse Madonna just as much as it can sanction Hillary Clinton) but the inter-relationship of masculinity and femininity in the public sphere remains a complex negotiation. What Western cultures have come to recognize and endorse as appropriate masculinity in the 1990s is different from that of the 1950s: when Sylvia Plath satirized conventional American masculinity in the form of Buddy Willard in *The Bell Jar* she was voicing the dissent of a generation of American women from the ideals of Eisenhower's America. Almost two decades later, those square-chinned heroes of the American space programme (the

objects of Tom Wolfe's satire in *The Right Stuff*) were seen by
W.H. Auden as the products of another, but no less undesirable,
form of American masculinity:

> It's natural the Boys should whoop it up for
> so huge a phallic triumph, an adventure
>   it would not have occurred to women
>   to think worth while, made possible only
>
> because we like huddling in gangs and knowing
> the exact time : yes, our sex may in fairness
>   hurrah the deed, although the motives
>   that primed it were somewhat less than
>   *menschlich.*[3]

Auden, Wolfe and Plath all represent – to different degrees and
with different emphasis – traditions of dissent with Western culture, and it is crucial to place that tradition on record since it is
all too easy to represent Western history as one long tale of tri-
umphant, uncontested masculinity. This feminist version of history is one that can be found, but it is a version that rightly has
received critical attention from diverse positions. Feminists have
pointed out the co-operation as well as the conflict between
women and men; male historians (particularly gay male historians) have pointed to the constant questioning and subversion of
conventional masculinity by gay men. (To this version of historical change Camille Paglia has added her own version of the past:
that without gay men there would be no Western cultural history.)[4] Writers from all these traditions have found in the past
rich evidence to suggest that there is no such thing, except in fantasy, of unproblematic, conventional, heterosexual masculinity.
No better example could display the gap between fantasy and
reality than the gradual recognition (achieved either by cultural
historians, biographers or individual revelation) that many of the
great heroes of the masculine in the Hollywood dream factory of
the 1950s were themselves gay or bisexual.[5]

The greater tolerance that the West now allows to both women
and men of increased freedom of public choice about private
behaviour can, therefore, be seen as one of the achievements of
the twentieth century. Clearly, this freedom is anything but

absolute (for example, the problematic relationship of gay men to the military remains in both Britain and the United States) but a degree of explicit toleration can be observed throughout the West. Indeed, sexual libertarianism has become part of the bench-mark of a 'modern' society: to maintain a public policy of homophobia is now equated with backwardness and illiberality. In this change, there has been much that has been positive for both sexes, not least in allowing women and men more public, and private, space for the determination of their individual sexualities.

Yet against this, or in the same context, we must set the other changes, and the other realities, of the twentieth century. Thus it is at this point – the concluding pages of this account of contemporary feminism – that we need to ask not just where contemporary feminism is in terms of its own arguments, priorities and agendas but where it is in terms of the world of the late twentieth century, and the degree to which feminism – and feminists – can claim to control its own (and their own) agenda. In a discussion of the 1995 Beijing conference Gayati Chakravorty Spivak put the point particularly bluntly when she spoke of the 'feminist status quo' continuing to provide an 'alibi for exploitation'.[6] In this point she was making explicit those reservations – mentioned earlier in this chapter – that many feminists (from both the North and the South) felt about the cultural domination of the United States. Nor, of course, is the United States simply culturally dominant, it is also economically the most powerful nation on earth. Even if that power and ascendancy no longer takes the same form as nineteenth-century economic power (when economic power and imperial domination went hand-in-hand) it nevertheless remains central to the ways in which all women live their lives.

It is at this point that there is a case for raising – however tentatively – the issue of the relationship between feminism and other accounts of the social world. Feminism, as already suggested in the previous pages, has built upon the theoretical insights of Freud, Marx and Foucault but the nature of the relationship between feminism and these traditions remains both problematic and uneasy. Feminism re-discovered Freud, just as it discovered Marx and grew up with Foucault, but in all these relationships there has been a complex issue of what feminism can take, and use, without compromising the integrity of feminism's agenda. What, however, has often been one sided in the relationship, is the extent to which feminism has transformed the major theoretical traditions of the West. To put this at its simplest: when women enter, as has happened, the academy, what difference does it make to theoretical accounts of the social and/or cultural world? Examples of the way in which feminist scholarship transforms the examination of particular authors (or texts or situations) are now extensive. More elusive is a transformation of, for example, the theory of surplus value or the unconscious. Thus at the level of abstraction, of theoretical accounts of the world that can be used to offer general explanations of our social and cultural world, we have to ask how far feminism can take us, before encountering not difference, but similarity in the experiences of women and men. What then becomes crucial is both maintaining the difference that gender can make (in literal and symbolic ways) and yet not creating a feminism of politics of identity, within which as E.J. Hobsbawm has suggested, 'identity groups are about themselves, for themselves, and nobody else.'[7]

That feminism has already made a difference to the academic understanding of the lives of women can be demonstrated by any reading of contemporary Western sociological literature on the family. To take just one example: Anthony Giddens's *The Transformation of Intimacy* put forward a case about the changing nature of personal relations in the West that drew very extensively on recent feminist literature. Yet as persuasive and sympathetic as the book was on such issues as the unequal division of power in marriage and male violence against women, two features of the book are striking to a feminist reader. The first is that in terms of the sexual division of labour in the book it is women who offer the descriptions of conventional marriage and heterosexuality and men who offer the analysis. As the book proceeds to its conclusion, so women disappear and men take over. The second striking feature – and here it is in the book's conclusion – is that Giddens links the emergence of what he sees as more 'democratic' relations between women and men with the emergence of more democratic social relations in general. On that second point the jury must remain out: there is a strong case to put that those more 'democratic' relations between women and men of which Giddens speaks are being achieved, at least in part, because of the breakdown of male employment, rather than individually negotiated contracts. However unpalatable it may be to post-Marxists, it may be (yet again) that material conditions are determining consciousness rather than the reverse.[8]

Exactly what is changing in male/female relationships in the West remains contentious. There is some evidence to support the idea of more autonomy amongst women, but little to support the idea of the 'new men' so beloved of the media. But what we can see in Giddens's book is a way of looking at the world that has changed little for decades – a way that supposes that explanation and/or analysis is in some way more 'real' when achieved by men. Thus the organizing structure of *The Transformation of Intimacy* is, in many ways, not all that different from Dorothy Sayers's *Gaudy Night*. In that novel Sayers's heroine, Harriet Vane, returns to her Oxford college – a community of women – to investigate some mysterious and unpleasant events. What she discovers is that within this community are a series of difficult and rivalrous relationships between women. The events become more and more unpleasant, and Harriet is eventually forced to turn to her male suitor – Peter Wimsey – to come and discover what is going on. The final, terrible, disclosure of the novel is that the 'villain' of the story is a woman: a woman whose husband has had his academic reputation ruined by one of the women dons. In a speech that follows Peter Wimsey's disclosure of the culprit's identity, the guilty woman says:

> A woman's job is to look after a husband and children. I wish I had killed you. I wish I could kill you. I wish I could burn down this place and all the places like it – where you teach women to take men's jobs and rob them first and kill them afterwards.[9]

The accusation, with all its implications of the unsuitability of women for the academy, and the 'unnatural' community created by women academics, is hardly surprising – given that throughout the novel there has been a consistent ambivalence about the relationship of women to knowledge and the academy. A reader can hardly fail to notice that the novel ends with Harriet's agreement to marry Peter Wimsey: a tacit acknowledgement that whatever Harriet's strengths she cannot manage without Peter. Equally, throughout the novel there has been an implicit critique of feminism: the character whom Harriet most dislikes is a feminist and there is little suggestion that what women have to offer the academy is anything but a pale reflection of male scholarship. There are positive women characters, but they are positive as much through their conformity as their non-conformity. *Gaudy Night* was first published in 1935 and as such it can hardly be seen as part of contemporary fiction. But what it does represent are two continuing traditions within the twentieth century: the uneasy relationship of women to the *authority* of knowledge and the perception of the difficulties that women have of acting autonomously without male support. For example, in much detective fiction written by women in the 1960s and the 1970s (and the *genre* has remained consistently attractive both for women readers and women writers) the woman detective (however independent and competent) has frequently to call on male support and assistance. In the case of male detectives, the balance is different: the inspired, sensitive and yet often unconventional male detective is balanced by a male colleague who represents conventional masculinity. From Dr Watson in Conan Doyle to Sergeant Lewis in Colin Dexter, this pattern has held as the effective strategy of discovery.

Detective fiction is not, of course, absolutely comparable to the subject matter of the academy. Nevertheless, the project of discovery around which the work of the academy must revolve is in many ways similar to the work of the uncovering of crime. The academy is not scattered, at least literally, with dead bodies, but the process of the accumulation of knowledge does depend, as Thomas Kuhn and others have pointed out, on the overthrow of theories and the symbolic consignment to death of discarded ideas and practices. In this process and in this relationship, women have to overcome not only the usual difficulties of combining academic work with conventional expectations of femininity, but also establish a theoretical position that overcomes the

133

inherent universalism of much theoretical work and assert the difference of the feminine, within a social world in which the distinct responsibilities of femininity are considerable. It is not just a double shift – it involves a triple shift of balancing the reality of womanhood, its diverse literal and symbolic constructions and the social world within which women construct their identities. In all this, what women have to confront is the difficulty of avoiding what Henrietta Moore has described as 'master narratives'. Writing about the relationship of the male anthropologist to his text she remarks:

> while early anthropology was influenced by travel writing, it was also influenced by the Victorian 'boys own' story in which the central theme is a heroic white man penetrating a dark continent at great personal risk: Rider Haggard's *King Solomon's Mines*, John Buchan's *Prester John* and many others. Anthropological imaginative discourse drew both on Romantic themes about the novel savage in Paradise and on the heroic guests of the adventure story genre.[10]

In the discussion that follows this remark, what Henrietta Moore does is to show the remarkably close relationship between the imaginative world of male anthropologists (the world of the fiction and the cultural myths that they grew up with) and their accounts of the various societies subjected to anthropological examination. The structure of the imagination is already in place, she suggests, before any anthropologist sets off for his (or indeed her) field work.

But here we arrive at the crucial problem for feminism in the late twentieth century. Moore, and others, can point out the way in which the perception of male anthropologists of societies other than their own was influenced by the world from which they came, but we have to consider that the same might be true for women. As Moore herself says, in the chapter that follows her account of 'master narratives':

> What role do the symbolic and the fictive play in the setting up of a model about the so called real? These are not new thoughts, in fact they are rather old ones, but the general point remains in relation to my discussion of feminism and anthropology. What part do

the fictional and the symbolic play in setting up our intellectual models of the world, a world we assume to be real?[11]

Hence whilst feminism can recognize (and has very forcefully both recognized and revealed) many of the assumptions underlying theoretical accounts of the world as founded in male expectations and experiences it has still to continue to confront the question of the relationship of feminism to Western (and indeed masculinist) values of individualism. The 'whiteness' of much of Western feminism has been very fully contested and criticized by women of colour, but many women still voice the suspicion – first made in the nineteenth century – that feminism is essentially for, and about, middle-class women who aspire to patterns of autonomy familiar to middle-class men. For example, the conclusion to Simone de Beauvoir's *The Second Sex* (probably the greatest feminist work of the twentieth century) calls upon women to accept masculine values, to take and to act in the same ways as men. As a perceptive critic has pointed out:

> It is surely a bleak prospect. The emancipated woman sounds just like that familiar nineteenth century character, the self-made man. And isn't that the model underlying her philosophical sophistication? Early capitalist man, dominating and exploiting the natural world, living to produce, viewing his own life as a product shaped by will, and suppressing those elements in himself – irrationality, sexuality – that might reduce his moral and economic efficiency. His moral and emotional life is seen in capitalist terms – as de Beauvoir tends to see hers.[12]

The Second Sex was first published in 1949 and since that time new discourses about sexuality have much extended the options open to women – not the least of which is, in the West, the public choice of a lesbian identity. Equally, the bourgeois codes and conventions (of dress, manners and behaviour) against which de Beauvoir spent much of her life rebelling have been either undermined or liberalized. Yet at the same time, what has also happened to the West as a whole is that a new form of culture – of consumerism and consumption – has come to replace the more restrictive form of capitalism within which de Beauvoir grew up. But – and it is a qualification of the utmost importance – this shift in the emphasis of capitalism takes place against a global picture in which the growing gap between countries of the North and South in terms of standard of living offers endless opportunities for political and social de-stabilization. Pessimistic theories about the future have long been a feature of the West in the twentieth century (and seem to flourish particularly clearly at millennial points) but these theories and ideas about the world, and the social and economic relations within it, are nevertheless an important part of the context of contemporary feminism. A recognition of the realities of the contemporary world provides two essential services for feminism. First, it allows us to recognize (and to continue to recognize) the differences in material circumstances between women (within societies and between societies). Second, it allows us to consider that the value of 'difference' that is so central to contemporary Western feminism can also be analogous to differences available to consumers; that is, the apparent range of consumer options is limited in crucial ways that cannot be changed by consumer 'choice'.

The response of contemporary feminism to these issues has so far largely centred around ecology and the most abusive form of masculinity, which is the military. The case of Greenham Common is just one instance of the way in which women have attempted, as women, and through an explicit definition of womenhood as different from masculinity, to resist a specific form of military politics. Nevertheless, that resistance, and the form of resistance has met considerable feminist resistance in the assumptions that are made about 'good women' and 'bad men'. Reviewing the literature on the issue – and the related issue of essentialism – Caroline New has pointed out that:

> Social constructionist and de-constructionist feminists have trouble with the categories of 'women' and 'female' as evidenced by Wittig's claim that 'lesbians are not women'. For Haraway there is nothing about being 'female' that naturally binds women. There is not even such a state as 'being' female, itself a highly complex category constructed in contested sexual scientific discourse and other social practices. For Butler, sexed bodies are constructed as such retrospectively, from the standpoint of already dichotomized gender – that is, intersexed bodies are constructed, linguistically and medically, as male or female.[13]

But, New goes on to argue that, in her view, sexual differences are real, and have an impact on social organization that is crucial. Defending herself against a charge of essentialism she remarks that the trouble with essentialism is 'not its realism, but its lack of depth and its simplification of causal processes.'[14] Putting together a case for a more sophisticated essentialism – and certainly one that allows for social hierarchy and subordination – she points out that women, like men, have a complex relationship to both social change (and female emancipation) and the defence of the *status quo*. As she might have gone on to point out, the recognition of social differences does not necessarily involve the re-distribution of social power.

Indeed, one of the accusations against certain versions of feminism is that far from being an agent for change, it is an agent for stabilization. As Nancy Hartsock has pointed out:

> Men's power to structure social relations in their own image means that women too must participate in social relations which manifest and express abstract masculinity.[15]

The quotation vividly sums up what must be the shared experience of many women working in areas dominated by men: that often the only viable form of participation for women in public life is the replication of male behaviour. Indeed, a version of feminism, and feminist history, has been to campaign for entry, *on similar terms*, to institutions or professions previously open only to men. To take the most extreme example: women entering the military in the United States have campaigned for the right for full participation in military life, up to and including the right to kill. It is fortunate that very few people, let alone many women, view this career with great favour; nevertheless, what the example demonstrates is the *possible* direction of a version of feminism.

But at the same time as a (few) women campaign for full participation in the more unattractive manifestations of traditional masculinity, many other women campaign against militarism, the destruction of the environment and the specific injustices and cruelties attached to the condition of woman. They do so in the face of a culture that tends – and has always tended – towards the prioritization of the interests of the most socially and materially powerful. No society in the West, however stable and enlightened its government and policies might be, actually invites dissent, disruption and difference. When W.H. Auden wrote *Under which Lyre: A Reactionary Tract for the Times* he set up a conflict between 'the sons of Hermes' and 'Apollo's Children' in which the former, dreary children of the machine age, love to rule and personify all that is most conventional about public men. Teasingly, Auden continues:

> And when he occupies a college,
> Truth is replaced by Useful Knowledge;
> He pays particular
> Attention to Commercial thought,
> Public Relations, Hygiene, Sport,
> In his curricula.[16]

What women – through feminism – now claim, is more space free of that 'Useful Knowledge' of the market economy. The realization of the possibilities of the emancipation of women, recognized so clearly by Mary Wollstonecraft in 1792 is not, therefore, just about access to participation in the existing world, but participation in the transformation of it in ways that give some hope to the realization of human equality. In making clear the difference of woman, contemporary feminism has the opportunity to demonstrate the difference that women can make.

Notes

Introduction

1 Audré Lorde, 'The Master's Tools', pp. 110–13.
2 I am indebted to Pat Macpherson and Anne Seller for their discussion of this point.
3 Carole Pateman, *The Sexual Contract* and Sasha Roseneil *Disarming Patriarchy. Feminism and Political Action at Greenham.*

Chapter 1 Enter Women

1 Philip Larkin, *Annus Mirabilis*, in his *Collected Poems*, p. 167.
2 Jeffrey Weeks is amongst those who have catalogued, and theorized, the changing sexual codes of the 1960s. See Jeffrey Weeks, *Sex, Politics and Society*. His account of the 'sexual revolution' is contested by other writers – notably Sheila Jeffreys – as discussion later in this chapter suggests.
3 See Ernest Mandel, 'Where is America Going?', pp. 3–15.
4 The links between the struggles in France and those in the United States were made, for example, in a special issue of *New Left Review* entitled 'Festival of the Oppressed'. *New Left Review*, No. 52, 1968.

5 Sara Davidson, *Loose Change.*
6 Sheila Rowbotham's first works were *Hidden from History* and *Women's Consciousness, Man's World.* Subsequent works have included studies of women outside the West and on the relationship of feminism to socialism: *Women, Resistance and Revolution* and, with Lynne Segal and Hilary Wainwright, *Beyond the Fragments.*
7 Mary Wollstonecraft's *A Vindication of the Rights of Woman* was first published in 1792, Simone de Beauvoir's *The Second Sex* in 1949.
8 See Germaine Greer, *The Female Eunuch*; Kate Millett, *Sexual Politics*; Shulamith Firestone, *The Dialectic of Sex.* Two of these works – those of Millett and Figes, explicitly acknowledge their debt to de Beauvoir.
9 An explicit identification to be found in *Flying*, Millett's autobiographical account of feminist stardom and coming out as a lesbian.
10 The best example of these links is that Kate Millett's *Sexual Politics* was originally a doctoral thesis at New York's Columbia University.
11 Robin Morgan, *Sisterhood is Powerful* was followed by *Sisterhood is Global.*
12 This argument was originally put by Engels in 1884 in *The Origin of the Family, Private Property and the State.* For a discussion of the relationship of this work to feminism see J. Sayers, M. Evans and N. Redclift (eds), *Engels Re-Visited.*
13 See, in particular, Sheila Jeffreys, *Anticlimax* and Mary Daly, *Gyn/Ecology: The Metaethics of Radical Feminism.*
14 As early as 1977, voices had been raised about the problem of the category of 'women'. See Felicity Edholm, Olivia Harris and Kate Young, 'Conceptualising Women', pp. 101–30.
15 The issues about Gender Studies and Women's Studies are discussed in Jane Aaron and Sylvia Walby (eds), *Out of the Margins.*
16 It also has to be said here that it is Women's Studies, and not Gender Studies, which has thrived, in terms of both intellectual vitality and interest.
17 See the collection edited by the Feminist Review collective, *Waged Work.*
18 Ann Oakley, *Housewife.*
19 Christine Delphy, *The Main Enemy: A Materialist Analysis of Women's Oppression.* See too the comments by Michèle Barrett and Mary McIntosh, 'Christine Delphy: Towards a Materialist Feminism?', pp. 95–106.
20 See Hilary Land, 'The Myth of the Male Breadwinner', and Arlie Hochschild, *The Second Shift.*
21 Particularly significant was the contribution made by Veronica

Beechey (in Feminist Review collective, *Waged Work*) and Anne Phillips and Barbara Taylor on 'Sex and Skill', pp. 79–88.

22 Crucial works by these figures were Adrienne Rich's *Of Woman Born*, Audré Lorde's *Sister Outsider*, Hélène Cixous's 'The Laugh of the Medusa', pp. 196–206 and Luce Irigaray's 'When Our Lips Speak Together'.

23 See Maggie Humm, *Feminisms*, pp. 54–5.

24 The fullest discussion of the use of the term is to be found in Sylvia Walby, *Theorising Patriarchy*.

25 See Carol Smart, *The Ties That Bind: Law, Marriage and the Reproduction of Patriarchal Relations*.

26 Sheila Rowbotham, 'The Trouble with Patriarchy', pp. 364–70.

27 C.W. Mills, *Power, Politics and People*, pp. 339–46.

28 Peter Willmott's *Adolescent Boys of East London* is a particularly good example of this assumption of the public world.

29 Talal Asad (ed.), *Anthropology and the Colonial Encounter* (London, Ithaca Press, 1975).

30 Hazel Carby, 'White Women Listen!', p. 232.

31 A most useful introduction to post-modern understanding is given in David Harvey, *The Condition of Post Modernity*.

32 See, for example, the essays in the collection edited by Carole Vance, *Pleasure and Danger: Exploring Female Sexuality*.

33 See Celia Kitzinger, *The Social Construction of Lesbianism*, and Jeffrey Weeks, *Sexuality and its Discontents*.

34 Elizabeth Cowie, 'Woman as Sign', pp. 49–63.

35 The work of both writers has been edited and introduced by British feminists. See Jacqueline Rose and Juliet Mitchell (eds) *Feminine Sexuality – Jacques Lacan and the Ecole Freudienne* and Toril Moi (ed.) *The Kristeva Reader*.

Chapter 2 Public and Private: Women and the State

1 This thesis – that the family is a place of secrecy – was explicit in *The Anti-Social Family*, by Michèle Barrett and Mary McIntosh.

2 Linda Colley, *Britons: Forging the Nation*.

3 See Pippa Norris and Joni Lovenduski, *Political Recruitment: Gender, Race and Class in the British Parliament*.

4 This is particularly so in the case of participation in formal public politics: the debates about quotas for women candidates in the British Labour Party suggests the degree of resistance by men to *explicit* attempts to re-distribute public power.

5 Jane Austen, *Persuasion*, p. 237.

6   Mary Wollstonecraft, quoted in Virginia Sapiro, *A Vindication of Political Virtue*, p. 179.
7   Ibid., quoting Mary Wollstonecraft, p. 179.
8   Jane Humphries, 'Protective Legislation', pp. 1–33.
9   For example, Hilary Land, 'The Family Wage'.
10 One of the more important campaigns on this issue was that led by Josephine Butler in Britain against the infamous Contagious Diseases Act. See Judith Walkowitz, *Prostitution and Victorian Society*.
11 Anna Davin, 'Imperialism and Motherhood'.
12 This view has been put, most famously, by Arthur Marwick in *Britain in the Century of Total War*.
13 See Elizabeth Wilson, *Women and the Welfare State*.
14 Mary McIntosh, 'The State of the Oppression of Women', pp. 303–33.
15 Beatrix Campbell, *Goliath*.
16 Barbara Ehrenreich, *The Hearts of Men*.
17 Zillah Eisenstein, 'Eastern European Male Democracies'.
18 See Maxine Molyneux, 'The Woman Question and Communism's Collapse' and Barbara Einhorn, *Cinderella Goes to Market*.
19 Janet Hadley, 'God's Bullies: Attacks on Abortion', p. 97.
20 Lama Abu Odeh, 'Postcolonial Feminism and the Veil'.
21 Michel Foucault, *The Birth of the Clinic*, p. 31.
22 A number of studies of Foucault and feminism have now been published. See, for example Louis McNay, *Foucault and Feminism* and Caroline Ramazanoglu (ed.), *Up Against Foucault*.
23 Louis Althusser, 'Ideology and Ideological State Apparatuses', in *Lenin and Philosophy*, pp. 121–70.
24 Linda Gordon, *Heroes of their Own Lives* and Hilary Graham 'Surviving by Smoking'.
25 See Jennifer Temkin, 'Women, Rape and Law Reform' and Carol Smart 'Unquestionably a Moral Issue'.
26 Martha Nussbawm, 'Justice for Women', pp. 328–40, quotation on p. 337.
27 Barbara Ehrenreich and Deirdre English, *For Her Own Good*.
28 Londa Schiebinger, *The Mind Has No Sex*.
29 This point, about the possible instabilities of gender characteristics is discussed by Henrietta Moore in 'Sex, Gender and Sexual Difference'.
30 The difference between Britain and Germany is discussed in Claudia Koonz, *Mothers in the Fatherland*.
31 See Denise Riley, *War in the Nursery* and on the 1950s in Britain, Elizabeth Wilson, *Only Half-Way to Paradise*.
32 Meg Stacey, 'Feminist Reflections on the General Medical Council'.

33 Ibid., p. 185.
34 Various collections illustrate this literature. See, for example, Sandra Acker, *Gendered Education*, and Valerie Walkerdine, *Counting Girls Out*.
35 C. Luke and J. Gore (eds), 'Women in the Academy'.
36 Lisa Adkins, *Gendered Work*, Annie Phizacklea, 'Gender, Racism and Occupational Segregation' and Linda McDowell, 'Gender Divisions in a Post-Fordist Era'.
37 Gayatri Spivak, *Outside in the Teaching Machine*.
38 Avtar Brah, 'Re-framing Europe, p. 12.

Chapter 3 Engendering Knowledge

1 See the account given by de Beauvoir herself in the fourth volume of her autobiography, *All Said and Done*, pp. 479–95.
2 De Beauvoir's epistemology is discussed by Sonia Kruks in 'Gender and Subjectivity'.
3 Simone de Beauvoir, *All Said and Done*, p. 494.
4 Dale Spender, *Man Made Language*.
5 Useful accounts of the impact of Lacan and Derrida on feminist theory are given in Jacqueline Rose, *Sexuality in the Field of Vision*, pp. 18–23 and 49–81.
6 These texts are all published in Elaine Marks and Isabelle de Courtivron (eds), *New French Feminisms*. For commentaries on individual authors see Elizabeth Grosz, *Sexual Subversions* and Margaret Whitford, *Luce Irigaray*.
7 Janet Sayers, *Mothering Psychoanalysis*.
8 Jacqueline Rose and Juliet Mitchell (eds), *Feminine Sexuality – Jacques Lacan and the Ecole Freudienne*.
9 Janet Sayers, *Sexual Contradictions*, p. 86.
10 Julia Kristeva, 'Warnings', p. 136.
11 Ibid., p. 136.
12 Simone de Beauvoir, *The Second Sex*, p. 249.
13 See, for example, J. Nicholson, *Men and Women*.
14 Adrienne Rich, quoted in Janet Sayers, *Sexual Contradictions*, p. 42.
15 Mary Daly, *Gyn/Ecology*.
16 See Judith Butler, in particular, in *Gender Trouble* and *Bodies that Matter*.
17 Mary Shelley, *Frankenstein*, p. 145.
18 Londa Schiebinger, *The Mind has No Sex*.
19 Alice Rossi, 'Women in Science'.
20 Sandra Harding, *The Science Question in Feminism*, p. 142.
21 Ibid., p. 117.

22 Ibid, p. 117.
23 See Ludmilla Jordanova, *Sexual Visions* and Evelyn Fox Keller, *Reflections on Gender and Science.*
24 Elizabeth Fee, 'Is Feminism a Threat to Scientific Objectivity?'.
25 Hannah Gavron, *The Captive Wife*, Betty Friedan, *The Feminine Mystique*, Ann Oakley, *Housewife*, Sally Alexander, 'Women's Work in Nineteenth Century London', Sheila Rowbotham, *Hidden from History* and Joan Scott and Louise Tilly, 'Women's Work and Family in Nineteenth Century Europe'.
26 See Irene Bruegel, 'Sex and Race in the Labour Market' and Veronica Beechey, 'Some Notes on Female Wage Labour in Capitalist Production'.
27 Charlotte Brontë, *Jane Eyre*, p. 128.
28 Socialist feminist history is now fully represented in *History Workshop Journal*, even if it does not always figure quite so prominently in university departments of history.
29 An account of the richness of Black feminism is given by Patricia Hill Collins in 'Black feminist thought'.
30 See Jean Rhys, *Wide Sargasso Sea*, Elaine Showalter, *The Female Malady* and Sandra Gilbert and Susan Gubar, *The Madwoman in the Attic.*
31 See, for example, L.J. Walker, 'Sex Differences in the Development of Moral Reasoning'.
32 Alison Jaggar, *Feminist Politics and Human Nature*, pp. 384–5.

Chapter 4 Representation

1 See the article by Rebecca O'Rourke, 'Summer Reading'.
2 A useful account of the importance of the idea of tradition to F.R. Leavis is given in Alan Swingewood, *Sociological Poetics and Aesthetic Theory*, pp. 109–13. A feminist reading of F.R. Leavis is given by Catherine Belsey in 'Re-reading the Great Tradition'.
3 Georg Lukács is best known for his *The Historical Novel* and *The Meaning of Contemporary Realism.*
4 There is no one collection of Orwell's literary criticism; it appears in the four volumes of *The Collected Essays, Journalism and Letters of George Orwell.*
5 For example, see Elaine Showalter, *Sexual Anarchy.*
6 Class politics in the novel – and particularly the English novel – were discussed by Arnold Kettle in *An Introduction to the English Novel* and Raymond Williams, *The Long Revolution.*
7 See 'Victims and Victors', in Elizabeth Hardwick's *Seduction and Betrayal*, pp. 91–145.

8   It is, however, important to point out that in her most recent work
    Germaine Greer has come close to suggesting that much literary
    work by women (in particular poetry) *is* actually definable as sec-
    ond rate. See Germaine Greer, *Slipshod Sibyls*.
9   Kenneth Clark, *The Nude*.
10 Julia Kristeva, 'Women's Time'.
11 Janet Woolf, *Feminine Sentences*, p. 73.
12 See the discussion of Mary Kelly in Janet Woolf, *Feminine
    Sentences*, pp. 94–7.
13 See Catherine Belsey, *Critical Practice*.
14 Janet Woolf, *Feminine Sentences*, p. 69.
15 Terry Eagleton, *The Rape of Clarissa*.
16 Elaine Showalter (ed.), *The New Feminist Criticism*.
17 See David Frisby, *Fragments of Modernity*.
18 Elizabeth Wilson, *The Sphinx in the City* and Rachel Bowlby, *Just
    Looking*.
19 Cora Kaplan, 'Radical Feminism and Literature', p. 14.
20 See the account by Elizabeth Wilson, 'The Barnard Conference on
    Sexuality'.
21 Ros Coward, 'Are Women's Novels Feminist Novels?', p. 55.
22 Ibid., p. 57.
23 Toril Moi, *Sexual/Textual Politics*, p. 87.
23 Nancy K. Miller, *The Heroine's Text*.
24 Tony Tanner, *Adultery in the Novel*.
25 See Elaine Showalter's *Sexual Anarchy* and Sandra Gilbert and
    Susan Gubar, *No Man's Land* and Ann Douglas, *The Feminization
    of American Culture*.
26 Nancy Armstrong, *Desire and Domestic Fiction*, p. 11.
27 Elizabeth Cowie, 'Woman as Sign'. See too Denise Riley, *Am I That
    Name?*. In the context of the academic study of history, Joan Scott has
    raised similar questions about the limits of the term 'women' in histor-
    ical research. See Joan Scott, *Gender and the Politics of History*.
28 Eve Kosofsky Sedgwick, *Between Men* and *Epistemology of the
    Closet*.
29 The argument against pornography is put most forcefully by
    Andrea Dworkin. See 'Interview with Andrea Dworkin'.
30 Although the major focus of feminist critics was the novel, there
    were important studies of other literary forms. See, for example Jan
    Montefiore, *Feminism and Poetry*.
31 See Jackie Stacey (ed., with Lynne Pearce), *Romance Revisited*,
    Judith Williamson, *Decoding Advertisements*, Anne Kuhn,
    Women's Pictures.
32 See the collection edited by Linda Nicholson, *Feminism/
    Postmodernism*.

Chapter 5 The Body

1   See the essays in Linda Nicholson (ed.), *Feminism/Postmodernism* and Kate Soper, 'Feminism, Humanism and Postmodernism'.
2   Margery Spring-Rice, *Working Class Wives* and Margery Llewellyn Davies, *Life As We Have Known It*.
3   See Jeffrey Weeks, *Coming Out*, Sheila Jeffreys, *The Spinster and Her Enemies* and Lillian Faderman, *Surpassing the Love of Men*.
4   See, for example, Ed Cohen, *Talk on the Wilde Side* and Peter Middleton, *The Inward Gaze*.
5   Germaine Greer, *The Female Eunuch*.
6   Leeds Revolutionary Feminist Group, *Love Your Enemy?*, p. 6.
7   The reality of 'life within marriage' was explored in a considerable feminist literature in the 1970s and 1980s. See, for example Jan Pahl, 'Patterns of Money Management within Marriage', and for the United States, Lillian Rubin, *Worlds of Pain*.
8   Juliet Mitchell, *Psychoanalysis and Feminism*, Nancy Chodorow, *The Reproduction of Mothering* and Janet Sayers, *Biological Politics*.
9   Michel Foucault, quoted in David Macey, *The Lives of Michel Foucault*, p. 354.
10   Ibid., p. 358.
11   Alfred Kinsey, William Pomeroy and Clyde Martin, *Sexual Behaviour in the Human Male* and Michael Schofield, *The Sexual Life of Young Adults*. See the discussion in Liz Stanley, *Sex Surveyed, 1949–1994*.
12   Nancy Cott, 'Passionlessness' and Caroll Smith-Rosenberg, 'The Female World of Love and Ritual'.
13   'Editorial', *Signs*, Vol. 1, No. 1, Autumn 1975, p. v.
14   Carroll Smith-Rosenberg, 'The Female World of Love and Ritual', p. 29.
15   Nancy Cott, 'Passionlessness', p. 252.
16   Carol Christ, 'Victorian Masculinity and the Angel in the House'.
17   Homi Bhabha, *The Location of Culture*, pp. 66–93.
18   Liz Stanley (ed.), *The Diaries of Hannah Cullwick* and Rebecca Stott, 'The Dark Continent'.
19   Adrienne Rich, 'Compulsory Heterosexuality and Lesbian Existence', p. 633.
20   Elizabeth Wilson, 'The Barnard Conference on Sexuality'.
21   See, for example, Kathy Davis, *Re-shaping the Female Body*.
22   Elizabeth Fee, *Women and Health*, Ann Oakley, *The Captured Womb*. See too Adrienne Rich's passionate attack on the medicalization of childbirth, *Of Women Born* and Emily Martin on the

construction of the female body, particularly in gynaecology, as a site of failure and impairment.

23 Ros Coward, *Female Desire* and the essays in Carole Vance (ed.), *Pleasure and Danger*.
24 Judith Butler, *Gender Trouble*, pp. 7–8.
25 Judith Butler, *Gender Trouble*, p. 146.
26 Elizabeth Grosz, *Sexual Subversions* and *Volatile Bodies*.
27 Michelle Stanworth, *Reproductive Technologies* and Gena Corea and Renate Duelli-Klein (eds), *Man Made Women*.
28 See Elizabeth Grosz, *Sexual Subversions*, p. 27.
29 Particularly influential in recent years have been the ideas of what is described as 'queer theory'. Within this literature, Eve Kosofsky Sedgwick has made a notable contribution. On the issue of the merit of the absence of gender identity she has argued that instead of a fixed gender identity there should be 'an open mesh of possibilities, gaps, over-laps, dissonances and resonances, lapses and excesses of meaning when the constituent elements of anyone's gender, of anyone's sexuality aren't made (or can't be made) to signify monolithically. See Eve Kosofsky Sedgwick, *Epistemology of the Closet*, p. 28.
30 See S. Mitter, *Common Fate, Common Bond* and Maria Mies, *Patriarchy and Accumulation on a World Scale*.

Chapter 6 Feminism and the Academy

1 Elizabeth Wilson, 'Deviant Dress'.
2 See the discussion by Mandy Merckin, 'Bedroom Horror'.
3 See Nahid Yeganeh, 'Women, Nationalism and Islam in Contemporary Political Discourse in Iran'.
4 Elizabeth Grosz, *Sexual Subversions*, p. 33.
5 Elizabeth Grosz, *Sexual Subversions*, pp. 33–4.
6 A. Aziz, 'Women in U.K. Universities'.
7 Debbie Epstein, 'In Our (New) Right Minds'.
8 Andrea Spurling, *Report of the Women in Higher Education Project*.
9 See the essays by John Hoyles and Peter Brooker in Peter Widdowson (ed.), *Re-reading English*.
10 Noam Chomsky, *American Power and the New Mandarins*, E.P. Thompson, *Warwick University Ltd* and C.W. Mills, 'Knowledge'.
11 Janet Sayers, *The Man Who Never Was*, p. 214.
12 See Liz Kelly and Ruth Pearson, 'Women's Studies' and Dawn Currie and Hamida Kazi, 'Academic Feminism and the Process of De-radicalisation'.

13 Jalna Hanmer, (ed., with Mary Maynard), *Women, Violence and Social Control*, Catherine MacKinnon, *Towards a Feminist Theory of the State* and Ann Oakley, *The Captured Womb*.
14 Liz Stanley and Sue Wise, *Breaking Out*, p. 174.
15 See the work of Carolyn Steedman, for example, *Landscape for a Good Woman*, Carolyn Heilbrun, *Writing a Woman's Life* and Liz Stanley, *The Auto/Biographical I*.
16 Jacqueline Rose, 'Dora – Fragment of an Analysis', in *Sexuality in the Field of Vision*, pp. 27–48 and Toril Moi, 'Representation of Patriarchy: Sexuality and Epistemology in Freud's Dora'.
17 See Michèle Barrett and Anne Phillips, *Destabilizing Theory*.
18 Sandra Harding (ed.), *Feminism and Methodology*, p. 180.
19 Catherine Hall, *White, Male and Middle Class*, p. 257.

Chapter 7 Worlds of Difference

1   See for example, the discussion in Susan Faludi, *Backlash*.
2   Slavenka Drakulic, *How we Survived Communism and even Laughed*, p. 32.
3   W.H. Auden, *Selected Poems*, p. 294.
4   Camille Paglia, *Sexual Personae*.
5   See Corey Creekmur and Alexander Doty (eds), *Out in Culture* and Jackie Byars, *All that Hollywood Allows*.
6   Gayatri Chakravorty Spivak, 'Women as Theatre', p. 2.
7   E.J. Hobsbawm, 'Identity Politics and the Left'.
8   The links between gender and materialism have been extensively explored since the 1970s. See, from diverse theoretical perspectives, Annette Kuhn and Ann Marie Wolpe (eds), *Feminism and Materialism* and more recently Diana Leonard and Lisa Adkins (eds), *Sex in Question*.
9   Dorothy Sayers, *Gaudy Night*, p. 427.
10 Henrietta Moore, *A Passion for Difference*, p. 114.
11 Ibid., p. 139.
12 Margaret Walters, 'The rights and wrongs of women', p. 357.
13 Caroline New 'Man Bad – Woman Good?', p. 81.
14 Ibid.
15 Nancy Hartsock, 'The Feminist Standpoint', quoted in Ibid., p. 89.
16 W.H. Auden, *Under Which Lyre* in *Selected Poems*, p. 178.

Bibliography

Works consulted or cited in the text

Aaron, Jane and Walby, Sylvia, *Out of the Margins* (London, Falmer Press, 1991).

Acker, Sandra, *Gendered Education* (Milton Keynes, Open University Press, 1994).

Adkins, Lisa, *Gendered Work* (Milton Keynes, Open University Press, 1995).

Alexander, Sally, 'Women's Work in Nineteenth Century London', in Oakley, A. and Mitchell, J. (eds), *The Rights and Wrongs of Women* (Harmondsworth, Penguin, 1976), pp. 59–111.

Alther, Lisa, *Kinflicks* (London, Chatto, 1976).

Althusser, Louis, *Lenin and Philosophy* (London, New Left Books, 1971).

Angelou, Maya, *I Know Why the Caged Bird Sings* (New York, Random House, 1969).

Armstrong, Nancy, *Desire and Domestic Fiction* (Oxford, Oxford University Press, 1987).

Asad, Talal (ed.), *Anthropology and the Colonial Encounter* (London, Ithaca Press, 1975).

Auden, W.H., *Selected Poems* (London, Faber and Faber, 1979).

Austen, Jane, *Persuasion* (Harmondsworth, Penguin, 1965). First published in 1818.

Austen, Jane, *Mansfield Park* (Harmondsworth, Penguin, 1966). First published in 1814.

Bibliography

Aziz, A., 'Women in U.K. Universities', in Lie, S. and O'Leary, V. (eds), *Storming the Tower: Women in the Academic World* (London, Kogan Page, 1990).

Baker Miller, Jean, *Towards a New Psychology of Women* (Harmondsworth, Pelican, 1979).

Barrett, Michèle and McIntosh, Mary, 'Christine Delphy: Towards a Materialist Feminism?', *Feminist Review*, No. 1, 1979, pp. 95–106.

Barrett, Michèle and McIntosh, Mary, *The Anti-Social Family* (London, Verso, 1982).

Barrett, Michèle and Phillips, Anne (eds), *Destabilising Theory* (Cambridge, Polity Press, 1992).

Beauvoir, Simone de, *The Second Sex* (New York, Bantam Books, 1964). First published in 1949.

Beauvoir, Simone de, *All Said and Done* (Harmondsworth, Penguin, 1972).

Beechey, Veronica, 'Some Notes on Female Wage Labour in Capitalist Production', *Capital and Class*, No. 3, 1977, pp. 45–66.

Belsey, Catherine, *Critical Practice* (London, Methuen, 1980).

Belsey, Catherine, 'Re-reading the Great Tradition', in Widdowson, Peter (ed.), *Re-reading English* (London, Methuen, 1982), pp. 121–35.

Bhabha, Homi, *The Location of Culture* (London, Routledge, 1994).

Bowlby, Rachel, *Just Looking* (London, Methuen, 1985).

Brah, Artar, 'Re-framing Europe: Engendered Racisms, Ethnicities and Nationalisms in Contemporary Western Europe', *Feminist Review*, No. 45, 1993, pp. 9–28.

Bronfen, Elizabeth, *Over her Dead Body: Death, Femininity and the Aesthetic* (Manchester, Manchester University Press, 1992).

Brontë, Charlotte, *Jane Eyre* (London, Oxford University Press, 1961). First Published in 1847.

Brownmiller, Susan, *Against our Will* (New York, Simon and Schuster, 1975).

Bruegel, Irene, 'Sex and Race in the Labour Market', *Feminist Review*, No. 32, 1989, pp. 50–68.

Butler, Judith, *Gender Trouble* (London, Routledge, 1990).

Butler, Judith, *Bodies that Matter* (London, Routledge, 1993).

Byars, Jackie, *All that Hollywood Allows: Re-reading Gender in 1950s Melodrama* (London, Routledge, 1991).

Campbell, Beatrix, *Goliath* (London, Methuen, 1993).

Carby, Hazel, 'White Women Listen' in Centre for Contemporary Cultural Studies (ed.), *The Empire Strikes Back* (London, Hutchinson, 1984) pp. 212–36.

Castle, Terry, *The Apparitional Lesbian: Female Homosexuality and Modern Culture* (New York, Columbia University Press, 1993).

Chodorow, Nancy, *The Reproduction of Mothering* (Berkeley, University of California Press, 1978).

Chomsky, Noam, *American Power and The New Mandarins* (New York, Pantheon, 1969).

Christ, Carol, 'Victorian Masculinity and the Angel in the House', in Vicinus, Martha (ed.), *A Widening Sphere* (London, Methuen, 1977), pp. 146–62.

Christian, Barbara, *Black Women Novelists: The Development of a Tradition 1892–1976* (Westport, Greenwood Press, 1980).

Cixous, Hélène, 'The Laugh of the Medusa' in Humm, Maggie (ed.), *Feminisms* (Hemel Hempstead, Harvester, 1992), pp. 196–206.

Clark, Kenneth, *The Nude* (Harmondsworth, Penguin, 1960).

Cohen, Ed, *Talk on the Wilde Side* (London, Routledge, 1993).

Colley, Linda, *Britons: Forging the Nation* (Tiptree, Pimlico, 1996).

Corea, Gena and Duelli-Klein, Renate (eds), *Man Made Women: How New Reproductive Technologies Affect Women* (London, Hutchinson, 1985).

Cott, Nancy, 'Passionlessness: An Interpretation of Victorian Sexual Ideology', *Signs*, Vol. 4, No. 2, pp. 219–36.

Coward, Rosalind, 'Are Women's Novels Feminist Novels?', *Feminist Review*, No. 5, 1980, pp. 53–64.

Coward, Rosalind, *Patriarchal Precedents* (London, Routledge and Kegan Paul, 1983).

Coward, Rosalind, *Female Desire* (London, Paladin, 1984).

Cowie, Elizabeth, 'Woman as Sign', *M/F*, No. 1, 1978, pp. 49–63.

Creekmur, Corey and Doty, Alexander (eds), *Out in Culture: Gay, Lesbian and Queer Essays on Popular Culture* (London, Cassells, 1995).

Currie, Dawn and Kazi, Hamida, 'Academic Feminism and the Process of De-radicalisation', *Feminist Review*, No. 25, 1987, pp. 77–98.

Daly, Mary, *Gyn/Ecology: The Metaethics of Radical Feminism* (London, The Women's Press, 1979).

Davidson, Sara, *Loose Change* (New York, Simon and Schuster, 1977).

Davin, Anna, 'Imperialism and Motherhood', *History Workshop Journal*, No. 5, Spring 1978, pp. 9–65.

Davis, Kathy, *Re-shaping the Female Body: the Dilemma of Cosmetic Surgery* (London, Routledge, 1995).

Delphy, Christine, *The Main Enemy: A Materialist Analysis of Women's Oppression* (London WRRC Publications, No. 3, 1977).

Dinnerstein, Dorothy, *The Mermaid and the Minotaur* (New York, Harper and Row, 1976).

Douglas, Ann, *The Feminization of American Culture* (New York, Knopf, 1977).

Drakulic Slavenka, *How we Survived Communism and even Laughed* (London, Hutchinson, 1987).

151

Bibliography

Dworkin, Andrea, 'Interview with Andrea Dworkin', *Feminist Review*, No. 11, 1982, pp. 23–9.

Eagleton, Terry, *The Rape of Clarissa* (Oxford, Blackwell Publishers, 1982).

Edholm, Felicity, Harris, Olivia and Young, Kate, 'Conceptualising Women', *Critique of Anthropology*, Nos. 9/10, 1977, pp. 101–30.

Ehrenreich, Barbara and English, Deidre, *For Her Own Good: 150 Years of the Expert's Advice to Women* (London, Pluto, 1979).

Ehrenreich, Barbara, *The Hearts of Men: American Dreams and the Flight from Commitment* (London, Pluto, 1983).

Einhorn, Barbara, *Cinderella goes to Market* (London, Verso, 1993).

Eisenstein, Zillah, 'East European Male Democracies', in Frank, N. and Mueller, M. (eds), *Gender Politics and Post Communism* (London, Routledge, 1993), pp. 303–17.

Ellman, Mary, *Thinking about Women* (New York, Harcourt, 1968).

Engels, F., *The Origin of the Family, Private Property and the State* (Harmondsworth, Penguin, 1985).

Epstein, Debbie, 'In Our (New) Right Minds: The Hidden Curriculum and the Academy', in Morley, Louise and Walsh, Val (eds), *Feminist Academics on the Move* (London, Taylor and Francis, 1995), pp. 56–72.

Faderman, Lillian, *Surpassing the Love of Men* (London, The Women's Press, 1985).

Faludi, Susan, *Backlash* (London, Chatto and Windus, 1992).

Fee, Elizabeth, 'Is Feminism a Threat to Scientific Objectivity?' *International Journal of Women's Studies*, No. 4, 1981, pp. 378–92.

Fee, Elizabeth, *Women and Health: The Politics of Sex and Medicine* (New York, Baywood, 1983).

Feminist Review, *Waged Work* (London, Virago, 1986).

Firestone, Shulamith, *The Dialectic of Sex* (London, The Women's Press, 1979).

Foucault, Michel, *The Birth of the Clinic: An Archaeology of Medical Perception*, translated by Alan Sheridan Smith (London, Tavistock, 1973). Originally published as *La Naissance de la Clinique* (Paris, PUF, 1963).

Foucault, Michel, *The History of Sexuality Vol. 1: An Introduction*, translated by Robert Hurley (London, Allen Lane, 1979). Originally published as *Histoire de la Sexualité Vol. 1: La Volonté de Savoir* (Paris, Gallimard, 1976).

Fox Keller, Evelyn, *Reflections on Gender and Science* (New Haven, Yale University Press, 1985).

Freidan, Betty, *The Feminine Mystique* (New York, Norton, 1963).

Frisby, David, *Fragments of Modernity* (Cambridge, Polity Press, 1985).

Gardner, Katy, *Songs at the River's Edge: Stories from a Bangladeshi Village* (London, Virago, 1991).

Bibliography

Gavron, Hannah, *The Captive Wife* (London, Routledge and Kegan Paul, 1966).

Giddens, Anthony, *The Transformation of Intimacy* (Cambridge, Polity Press, 1993).

Gilbert, Sandra and Gubar, Susan, *The Madwoman in the Attic: The Woman Writer and the Nineteenth Century Literary Imagination* (New Haven, Yale University Press, 1984).

Gilbert, Sandra and Gubar, Susan, *No Man's Land* (New Haven, Yale University Press, 1988).

Gilligan, Carol, *In a Different Voice* (Cambridge, Harvard University Press, 1982).

Gordon, Linda, *Woman's Body, Woman's Right* (Harmondsworth, Penguin, 1977).

Gordon, Linda, *Heroes of their Own Lives* (London, Virago, 1989).

Graham, Hilary, 'Surviving by Smoking', in Wilkinson, Sue and Kitzinger, Celia (eds), *Women and Health* (London, Taylor and Francis, 1994), pp. 102–3.

Greer, Germaine, *The Female Eunuch* (London, MacGibbon and Kee, 1970).

Greer, Germaine, *The Obstacle Race* (London, Secker and Warburg, 1979).

Greer, Germaine, *Slipshod Sibyls* (London, Viking, 1995).

Griffiths, Morwenna and Whitford, Margaret (eds), *Feminist Perspectives in Philosophy* (London, Macmillan, 1988).

Grosz, Elizabeth, *Sexual Subversions* (London, Allen and Unwin, 1989).

Grosz, Elizabeth, *Volatile Bodies* (Bloomington, Indiana University Press, 1993).

Hadley, Janet, 'God's Bullies: Attacks on Abortion', *Feminist Review*, No. 48, 1994, p. 97.

Hall, Catherine, *White, Male and Middle Class* (Cambridge, Polity Press, 1992).

Hanmer, Jalna and Maynard, Mary (eds), *Women, Violence and Social Control* (London, Macmillan, 1987).

Harding, Sandra, *The Science Question in Feminism* (Milton Keynes, Open University Press, 1986).

Harding, Sandra (ed.), *Feminism and Methodology* (Milton Keynes, Open University Press, 1987).

Hardwick, Elizabeth, *Seduction and Betrayal* (New York, Vintage Books, 1975).

Harvey, David, *The Condition of Post Modernity* (Oxford, Blackwell Publishers, 1989).

Heilbrun, Carolyn, *Writing a Woman's Life* (London, Women's Press, 1988).

Hill Collins, Patricia, 'Black Feminist Thought', *Signs*, Vol. 14, No. 4, 1989, pp. 745–73.

Hobsbawm, E.J., 'Identity Politics and the Left', *New Left Review*, No. 217, 1996, pp. 38–47.

Hochschild, Archie, *The Second Shift* (New York, Viking, 1989).

Humm, Maggie, *Border Traffic* (Manchester, Manchester University Press, 1991).

Humm, Maggie (ed.), *Feminisms* (Hemel Hempstead, Harvester, 1992).

Humphries, Jane, 'Protective legislation, the Capitalist State and Working Class Men', *Feminist Review*, No. 7, 1981, pp. 1–33.

Irigaray, Luce, 'When Our Lips Speak Together', *Signs*, Vol. 6, No. 1, pp. 69–79.

Jaggar, Alison, *Feminist Politics and Human Nature* (Brighton, Harvester, 1983).

Jardine, Alice, *Gynesis: Configurations of Women and Modernity* (Ithaca, Cornell University Press, 1985).

Jeffreys, Sheila, *The Spinster and Her Enemies* (London, Pandora, 1985).

Jeffreys, Sheila, *Anticlimax* (London, The Women's Press, 1990).

Johnston, Jill, *Lesbian Nation* (New York, Simon and Schuster, 1973).

Jong, Erica, *Fear of Flying* (London, Hart-Davis, 1975).

Jordanova, Ludmilla, *Sexual Visions: Images of Gender in Science and Medicine between the Eighteenth and Twentieth Centuries* (Brighton, Harvester Wheatsheaf, 1989).

Kaluzynska, Eva, 'Wiping the Floor With Theory', *Feminist Review*, No. 6, 1980, pp. 27–54.

Kaplan, Cara, 'Radical Feminism and Literature: Rethinking Millett's Sexual Politics', *Red Letters*, No. 9, 1979, pp. 4–16.

Kelly, Liz and Pearson, Ruth, 'Women's Studies: Women Studying or Studying Women?', *Feminist Review*, No. 15, 1983, pp. 76–80.

Kelly, Mary, *Post Partum Document* (London, Routledge and Kegan Paul, 1983).

Kettle, Arnold, *An Introduction to the English Novel* (London, Hutchinson, 1967).

Kinsey, Alfred, Pomeroy, William and Martin, Clyde, *Sexual Behaviour in the Human Male* (Philadelphia, W.B. Saunders, 1978).

Kitzinger, Celia, *The Social Construction of Lesbianism* (London, Sage, 1987).

Klein, Viola, *The Feminist Character: History of an Ideology* (London, Routledge, 1989).

Komarovsky, Mirra, *Blue Collar Marriage* (New York, Vintage Books, 1962).

Koonz, Claudia, *Mothers in the Fatherland* (London, Methuen, 1986).

Kosofsky Sedgwick, Eve, *Between Men: English Literature and Male Homosocial Desire* (New York, Columbia Press, 1985).

Kosofsky Sedgwick, Eve, *Epistemology of the Closet* (Berkeley, University of California Press, 1991).

Bibliography

Kristeva, Julia, 'Warnings', in Marks, Elaine and de Courtivron, Isabelle (eds), *New French Feminisms* (Brighton, Harvester Wheatsheaf, 1981).

Kristeva, Julia, *Revolution in Poetic Language* (New York, Columbia University Press, 1984).

Kristeva, Julia, 'Women's Time', in Moi, Toril (ed.), *The Kristeva Reader* (Oxford, Blackwell Publishers, 1986), pp. 187–214.

Kruks, Sonia, 'Gender and Subjectivity: Simone de Beauvoir and Contemporary Feminism', *Signs*, Vol. 18, No. 1, 1992, pp. 89–110.

Kuhn, Annette and Wolpe, Anne Marie (eds), *Feminism and Materialism* (London, Routledge and Kegan Paul, 1978).

Kuhn, Annette, *Women's Pictures: Feminism and Cinema* (London, Routledge and Kegan Paul, 1982).

Land, Hilary, 'The Myth of the Male Breadwinner', *New Society*, 9th October 1975.

Land, Hilary, 'The Family Wage', *New Statesman*, 18th December 1981.

Larkin, Philip, *Collected Poems* (London, Faber, 1988).

Leavis, Q.D., *Fiction and the Reading Public* (London, Chatto and Windus, 1932).

Leeds Revolutionary Feminist Group, *Love Your Enemy? The Debate between Heterosexual Feminism and Political Lesbianism* (London, Only Women Press, 1981).

Leonard, Diana and Adkins, Lisa (eds), *Sex in Question: French Materialist Feminism* (London, Taylor and Francis, 1996).

Llewellyn Davies, Margaret, *Life As We Have Known It* (London, Virago, 1975). First published in 1931.

Lorde, Audré, 'The Master's Tools Will Never Dismantle the Master's House', in *Sister Outsider* (Trumansburg, Crossing Press, 1984), pp. 110–13.

Lukács, Georg, *The Historical Novel* (London, Merlin, 1962).

Lukács, Georg, *The Meaning of Contemporary Realism* (London, Merlin, 1963).

Luke, C. and Gore, J. (eds), 'Women in the Academy' in Luke, C. and Gore, J. (eds). *Feminisms and Critical Pedagogy* (New York, Routledge, 1992).

Lynd, Robert, *Knowledge for What?* (Princeton, Princeton University Press, 1939).

Macey, David, *The Lives of Michel Foucault* (London, Vintage, 1994).

MacKinnon, Catherine, *Towards a Feminist Theory of the State* (Cambridge, Harvard University Press, 1989).

Mandel, Ernest, 'Where is America Going?', *New Left Review*, No. 54, 1969, pp. 3–15.

Marks, Elaine and de Courtivron, Isabelle (eds), *New French Feminisms* (Brighton, Harvester, 1981).

Bibliography

Martin, Emily, *The Woman in the Body* (Milton Keynes, Open University Press, 1989).

Marwick, Arthur, *Britain in the Century of Total War: War, Peace and Social Change, 1900–1967* (London, The Bodley Head, 1968).

McDowell, Linda, 'Gender Divisions in a Post Fordist Era', in McDowell, L. and Pringle, R. (eds), *Defining Women* (Cambridge, Polity Press, 1992) pp. 181–93.

McIntosh, Mary, 'Who Needs Prostitutes? The Ideology of Male Sexual Needs', in Smart, Carole and Smart, Barry (eds), *Women, Sexuality and Social Control* (London, Routledge and Kegan Paul, 1978).

McIntosh, Mary, 'The State and the Oppression of Women', in Evans, Mary (ed.), *The Woman Question* (London, Fontana, 1982) pp. 303–33.

McNay, Louis, *Foucault and Feminism* (Cambridge, Polity Press, 1992).

Merckin, Mandy, 'Bedroom Horror', *Feminist Review*, Autumn 1988, pp. 89–103.

Metck, Mandy, 'Bedroom Horror', *Feminist Review*, Autumn 1988, No. 30, pp. 89–103.

Middleton, Peter, *The Inward Gaze: Masculinity and Subjectivity in Modern Culture* (London, Routledge, 1992).

Miles, Maria, *Patriarchy and Accumulation on a World Scale* (London, Zed Books, 1986).

Miller, Nancy K., *The Heroine's Text: Readings in the French and English Novel 1722–1792* (New York, Columbia University Press, 1980).

Millett, Kate, *Flying* (London, Hart-Davis, MacGibbon, 1975).

Millett, Kate, *Sita* (New York, Random House, 1976).

Millett, Kate, *Sexual Politics* (London, Virago, 1977).

Mills, C.W., 'Knowledge' in *Power, Politics and People* (Oxford, Oxford University Press, 1967), pp. 405–599.

Mitchell, Juliet, *Psychoanalysis and Feminism* (Harmondsworth, Penguin, 1974).

Mitter, S., *Common Fate, Common Bond* (London, Pluto, 1986).

Moers, Ellen, *A Literature of Their Own* (Princeton, Princeton University Press, 1977).

Moers, Ellen, *Literary Women* (London, The Women's Press, 1978).

Moi, Toril, 'Representation of Patriarchy: Sexuality and Epistemology in Freud's Dora', *Feminist Review*, No. 9, 1981, pp. 60–75.

Moi, Toril, *Sexual/Textual Politics* (London, Methuen, 1985).

Moi, Toril (ed.), *The Kristeva Reader* (Oxford, Blackwell Publishers, 1986).

Molyneux, Maxine, 'The Woman Question and Communism's Collapse', *New Left Review*, No. 183, 1990, pp. 23–49.

Montefiore, Jan, *Feminism and Poetry* (London, Pandora, 1987).

Bibliography

Moore, Henrietta, *A Passion for Difference* (Cambridge, Polity Press, 1994).

Moore, Henrietta, 'Sex, Gender and Sexual Difference', *Feminist Review*, No. 47, 1994, pp. 78–95.

Morgan, Robin, *Sisterhood is Powerful* (New York, Vintage Books, 1970).

Morgan, Robin, *Sisterhood is Global* (Harmondsworth, Penguin, 1984).

New, Caroline, 'Man Bad – Woman Good?', *New Left Review*, No. 216, 1996, pp. 79–93.

Nicholson, J., *Men and Women: How Different Are They?* (Oxford, Oxford University Press, 1984).

Nicholson, Linda (ed.), *Feminism/Postmodernism* (London, Routledge, 1990).

Norris, Pippa and Lovenduski, Joni, *Political Recruitment: Gender, Race and Class in the British Parliament* (Cambridge, Cambridge University Press, 1994).

Nussbawn, Martha, 'Justice for Women', *Women: A Cultural Review*, Vol. 4, No. 3, Winter 1993, pp. 328–40.

Oakley, Ann, *Housewife* (London, Allen Lane, 1974).

Oakley, Ann, *From Here to Maternity* (Harmondsworth, Penguin, 1981).

Oakley, Ann, *The Captured Womb: A History of the Medical Care of Pregnant Women* (Oxford, Blackwell Publishers, 1984).

Odeh, Abu Lama, 'Post colonial Feminism and the Veil: Thinking the Difference', *Feminist Review*, No. 43, 1993, pp. 26–37.

O'Rourke, Rebecca, 'Summer Reading', *Feminist Review*, No. 2, 1979, pp. 1–17.

Orwell, George, *The Collected Essays, Journalism and Letters of George Orwell* (Harmondsworth, Penguin, 1970).

Paglia, Camille, *Sexual Personae* (Harmondsworth, Penguin, 1992).

Pahl, Jan, 'Patterns of Money Management within Marriage', *Journal of Social Policy*, Vol. 9, No. 3, 1980, pp. 313–35.

Pateman, Carole, *The Sexual Contract* (Cambridge, Polity Press, 1988).

Phillips, Anne and Taylor, Barbara, 'Sex and Skill', *Feminist Review*, No. 6, 1980, pp. 79–88.

Phizacklea, Anne, 'Gender, Racism and Occupational Segregation', in Walby, S. (ed.) *Gender Segregation at Work* (Milton Keynes, Open University Press, 1988), pp. 43–54.

Pinchbeck, Ivy, *Women Workers in the Industrial Revolution* (Oxford, Oxford University Press, 1930).

Plath, Sylvia, *The Bell Jar* (London, Faber, 1963).

Ramazanoglu, Caroline (ed.), *Up Against Foucault: Some Tensions between Feminism and Foucault* (London, Routledge, 1993).

Bibliography

Rhys, Jean, *Wide Sargasso Sea* (London, André Deutsch, 1966).

Rich, Adrienne, *Of Woman Born* (London, Virago, 1979).

Rich, Adrienne, 'Compulsory Heterosexuality and Lesbian Existence', *Signs*, Vol. 5, No. 4, Summer 1980, pp. 631–60.

Riley, Denise, *War in the Nursery* (London, Virago, 1983).

Riley, Denise, *Am I That Name? Feminism and the Category of 'Women' in History* (Minneapolis, University of Minnesota Press, 1988).

Rose, Hilary, *Love, Power and Knowledge* (Cambridge, Polity Press, 1994).

Rose, Jacqueline, *Sexuality in the Field of Vision* (London, Verso, 1986).

Rose, Jacqueline, *The Haunting of Sylvia Plath* (London, Virago, 1991).

Rose, Jacqueline and Mitchell, Juliet (eds), *Feminine Sexuality – Jacques Lacan and the Ecole Freudienne* (London, Macmillan, 1982).

Roseneil, Sasha, *Disarming Patriarchy: Feminism and Political Action at Greenham* (Buckingham, Open University Press, 1995).

Rossi, Alice, 'Women in Science: Why So Few?', *Science*, 148, 1965, pp. 1196–202.

Rowbotham, Sheila, *Women, Resistance and Revolution* (London, Allen Lane, 1972).

Rowbotham, Sheila, *Hidden from History* (London, Pluto, 1973).

Rowbotham, Sheila, *Women's Consciousness, Man's World* (Harmondsworth, Penguin, 1973).

Rowbotham, Sheila, 'The Trouble with Patriarchy' in Raphael Samuel (ed.), *People's History and Socialist Theory* (London, Routledge and Kegan Paul, 1981), pp. 364–70.

Rowbotham, Sheila, Segal, Lynne and Wainwright, Hilary, *Beyond the Fragments* (London, Merlin, 1979).

Rubin, Lillian, *Worlds of Pain* (New York, Basic Books, 1976).

Sapiro, Virginia, *A Vindication of Political Virtue* (London, University of Chicago Press, 1992).

Sayers, Dorothy, *Gaudy Night* (London, Coronet, 1990).

Sayers, Janet, *Biological Politics* (London, Tavistock, 1982).

Sayers, Janet, *Sexual Contradictions* (London, Tavistock, 1986).

Sayers, Janet, *Mothering Psychoanalysis* (London, Hamish Hamilton, 1991).

Sayers, Janet, *The Man Who Never Was* (London, Chatto and Windus, 1995).

Sayers, Janet, Evans, Mary and Redclift, Nanneke (eds), *Engels Re-Visited* (London, Tavistock, 1987).

Sayre, Ann, *Rosalind Frankin and DNA: A Vivid View of What it is Like to be a Gifted Woman in an Especially Male Profession* (New York, Norton, 1975).

Bibliography

Schiebinger, Londa, *The Mind has No Sex* (Cambridge, Harvard University Press, 1989).

Schofield, Michael, *The Sexual Life of Young Adults* (London, Allen Lane, 1973).

Scott, Joan, *Gender and the Politics of History* (New York, Columbia University Press, 1988).

Scott, Joan and Tilly, Louise, 'Women's Work and the Family in Nineteenth Century Europe', *Comparative Studies in Society and History*, January, 1975, pp. 36–64.

Shelley, Mary, *Frankenstein* (Hertfordshire, Wordsworth Classics, 1994). First published in 1818.

Showalter, Elaine (ed.), *The New Feminist Criticism* (London, Virago, 1986).

Showalter, Elaine, *The Female Malady* (London, Virago, 1987).

Showalter, Elaine, *Sexual Anarchy: Gender and Culture at the Fin de Siècle* (London, Virago, 1992).

Smart, Carol, *The Ties That Bind: Law, Marriage and the Reproduction of Patriarchal Relations* (London, Routledge, 1984).

Smart, Carol, 'Unquestionably a Moral Issue: Rhetorical Devices and Regulatory Imperatives', in Segal, L. and McIntosh, M. (eds), *Sex Exposed* (London, Virago, 1992).

Smith-Rosenberg, Caroll, 'The Female World of Love and Ritual: Relations between Women in Nineteenth-Century America', *Signs* Vol. 1, No. 1, Autumn 1975, pp. 1–29.

Soper, Kate, 'Feminism, Humanism and Postmodernism', in Evans, Mary (ed.), *The Woman Question* (London, Sage, 1994).

Spender, Dale, *Man Made Language* (London, Pandora, 1980).

Spivak, Gayatri Chakravorty, *Outside in the Teaching Machine* (London, Routledge, 1993).

Spivak, Gayatri Chakravorty, 'Women as Theatre', *Radical Philosophy*, No. 75, 1996, p. 2.

Spring-Rice, Margery, *Working Class Wives* (Harmondsworth, Pelican, 1939).

Spurling, Andrea, *Report of the Women in Higher Education Project* (Cambridge, Kings College, 1990).

Stacey, Jackie (ed., with Pearce, Lynne), *Romance Revisited* (London, Lawrence and Wishart, 1995).

Stacey, Margaret and Price, Marion, *Women, Power and Politics* (London, Tavistock, 1981).

Stacey, Meg, 'Feminist Reflections on the General Medical Council', in Wilkinson, S. and Kitzinger, C. (eds), *Women and Health* (London, Taylor and Francis, 1994), pp. 181–203.

Stanley, Liz, *The Auto/Biographical I* (Manchester, Manchester University Press, 1992).

Bibliography

Stanley, Liz, *Sex Surveyed, 1949–1994* (London, Taylor and Francis, 1995).

Stanley, Liz (ed.), *The Diaries of Hannah Cullwick* (London, Virago, 1984).

Stanley, Liz and Wise, Sue, *Breaking Out: Feminist Consciousness and Feminist Research* (London, Routledge and Kegan Paul, 1983).

Stanworth, Michelle, *Reproductive Technologies: Gender, Motherhood and Medicine* (Cambridge, Polity Press, 1987).

Steedman, Carolyn, *Landscape for a Good Woman* (London, Virago, 1986).

Stott, Rebecca, 'The Dark Continent: Africa as Female Body in Haggard's Adventure Fiction', *Feminist Review*, No. 32, 1989, pp. 69–89.

Swingewood, Alan, *Sociological Poetics and Aesthetic Theory* (London, Macmillan, 1986).

Tanner, Tony, *Adultery in the Novel* (London, Johns Hopkins University Press, 1979).

Taylor, Barbara, 'The Men are as Bad as their Masters', *Feminist Studies*, Vol. 5, No. 1, 1979, pp. 7–40.

Taylor, Barbara, *Eve and the New Jerusalem* (London, Virago, 1983).

Temkin, Jennifer, 'Women, Rape and Law Reform', in Tomaselli, S. and Porter, R. (eds), *Rape: A Historical and Social Enquiry* (Oxford, Blackwell Publishers, 1986), pp. 16–40.

Thompson, E.P., *Warwick University Ltd.* (Harmondsworth, Penguin, 1970).

Vance, Carole (ed.), *Pleasure and Danger: Exploring Female Sexuality* (London, Pandora, 1992).

Walby, Sylvia, *Theorising Patriarchy* (Oxford, Blackwell Publishers, 1990).

Walker, Alice, *The Color Purple* (New York, Harcourt Brace Jovanovitch, 1983).

Walker, L.J., 'Sex Differences in the Development of Moral Reasoning: A Critical Review', *Child Development*, No. 55, 1984, pp. 677–92.

Walkerdine, Valerie, *Counting Girls Out* (London, Virago, 1989).

Walkowitz, Judith, *Prostitution and Victorian Society* (Cambridge, Cambridge University Press, 1980).

Walters, Margaret, 'The Rights and Wrongs of Women: Mary Wollstonecraft, Harriet Martineau and Simone de Beauvoir', in Oakley, Ann and Mitchell, Juliet (eds), *The Rights and Wrongs of Women* (Harmondsworth, Penguin, 1976), pp. 304–78.

Weeks, Jeffrey, *Coming Out: Homosexual Politics in Britain from the Nineteenth Century to the Present* (London, Quartet Books, 1977).

Weeks, Jeffrey, *Sex, Politics and Society* (London, Longman, 1981).

Bibliography

Weeks, Jeffrey, *Sexuality and its Discontents* (London, Routledge and Kegan Paul, 1985).

Weeks, Jeffrey, *Invented Moralities* (Cambridge, Polity Press, 1995).

Whitford, Margaret, *Luce Irigaray: Philosophy in the Feminine* (London, Routledge, 1991).

Widdowson, Peter (ed.), *Re-reading English* (London, Methuen, 1982).

Wilkinson, S. and Kitzinger, C. (eds), *Women and Health* (London, Taylor and Francis, 1994).

Williams, Raymond, *The Long Revolution* (Harmondsworth, Penguin, 1961).

Williamson, Judith, *Decoding Advertisements* (London, Marian Bryars, 1978).

Willmott, Peter, *Adolescent Boys of East London* (Harmondsworth, Penguin, 1966).

Wilson, Elizabeth, *Women and the Welfare State* (London, Tavistock, 1977).

Wilson, Elizabeth, *Only Half-Way to Paradise* (London, Tavistock, 1980).

Wilson, Elizabeth, 'The Barnard Conference on Sexuality', *Feminist Review*, No. 13, 1983, pp. 35–41.

Wilson, Elizabeth, *Adorned in Dreams* (London, Virago, 1985).

Wilson, Elizabeth, 'Deviant Dress', *Feminist Review*, Summer 1990, pp. 67–74.

Wilson, Elizabeth, *The Sphinx in the City* (London, Virago, 1991).

Wolfe, Tom, *The Right Stuff* (London, Faber, 1963).

Wollstonecraft, Mary, *A Vindication of the Rights of Woman* (London, Dent, 1970). First Published in 1792.

Woolf, Janet, *Feminine Sentences* (Cambridge, Polity Press, 1990).

Woolf, Virginia, *Orlando* (London, Grafton, 1977). First published in 1928.

Woolf, Virginia, *Three Guineas* (Oxford, Oxford University Press, 1992). First published in 1938.

Woolf, Virginia, *Mrs Dalloway* (Harmondsworth, Penguin, 1995). First published in 1925.

Yeganeh, Nahid, 'Women, Nationalism and Islam in Contemporary Political Discourse in Iran', *Feminist Review*, No. 44, 1993, pp. 3–18.

Index

Aaron, Jane 140n.15
abortion 12, 33–5, 63, 87, 98
Abortion Act (1967) 33, 34
academy
  authority/power 1–3, 19–20, 107,
    119
  femininity and 133–4
  feminism and 1, 4, 17–23, 24, 37,
    57, 58–9, 92–7, 101, 106–22,
    131
  masculine domination 19–20, 46,
    53, 55, 56, 58, 110–14
  student protest (1968) 6–7
Adkins, Lisa 43
advertising 71, 81, 84
Alexander, Sally 60
Alther, Lisa 57
Althusser, Louis 36
androgyny 32, 103, 108
Angelou, Maya 57, 83
anthropology 19, 52, 99, 119, 120,
  134
Armstrong, Nancy 80
arts, women in 65–84
Asad, Talal 19
Auden, W.H. 129, 138

Austen, Jane 25–7, 62, 70, 72
autobiography 120

Baker Miller, Jean 98
Barnard College, New York 75, 101,
  102
Barrett, Michèle 141n.1
Beauvoir, Simone de 2, 9, 19, 40,
  44–6, 47, 50, 100, 135
Beechey, Veronica 15, 60, 141n.21
Belsey, Catherine 72, 144n.2
Benjamin, Walter 74
Beveridge Report (1944) 29, 30, 31
biography 120
bisexuality 129
black feminism 61–2, 83
black women 99
  writers 68–9, 83
body 28, 39, 41, 50–2, 81, 85–105
Bosnia 124
Bowlby, Rachel 74
Brah, Avtar 43
Brittain, Vera 45
Bronfen, Elizabeth 102
Brontë, Charlotte 61, 62, 72
Brontë, Emily 72

Index

Brownmiller, Susan 35, 94
Bruegel, Irene 60
Bush, George 126
Butler, Josephine (author of *Gender Trouble*) 103–4, 136
Butler, Josephine (social reformer) 142n.10

Cambridge University 112
Campbell, Beatrix 30
capitalism 2–3, 30, 31, 126–7, 135
Carby, Hazel 20, 43, 61
Castle, Terry 79, 82
Chodorow, Nancy 91, 98, 99
Chomsky, Noam 113
Christian, Barbara 83
cinema 71, 81, 84, 103, 108
citizenship 3, 8, 14, 25, 26, 28
city life 74
Cixous, Hélène 15, 47, 49, 51
Clark, Kenneth 70
class 3, 9, 11, 12, 17, 25, 29, 77
  see also working class
Clinton, Hillary 127–8
Colley, Linda 25
colonialism 43, 62, 83
colour 17
  women of 12, 62, 97, 135
  see also black women
consumption, culture of 3, 31, 66, 135–6
contraception 5, 32, 34, 87, 97, 102
Corea, Gena 104
Cott, Nancy 94, 95, 96
Coward, Rosalind 60, 61, 74, 75–6, 102
Cowie, Elizabeth 81
Cullwick, Hannah 97
cultural studies 21, 66, 83
culture 9–10, 21, 83
  see also popular culture

Daly, Mary 11, 51, 52
Darwin, Charles 60, 113
Davidson, Sara 8
Davin, Anna 29, 61
Davis, Angela 61
de-construction 62, 64, 82

de-constructionist feminism 136
Delphy, Christine 14
Derrida, Jacques 47, 108, 110, 121
desire *see* sexual desire
Deutsch, Hélène 48
difference 2
  between men's and women's worlds 123–38
  between women 11, 17, 20, 62–3, 136
  see also gender difference; sexual difference
Dinnerstein, Dorothy 98
dissent, traditions of 2, 40, 128–9
diversity 63, 78, 117
divorce 31, 37
domestic work 14, 19, 60
Douglas, Ann 80
Drakulic, Slavenka 125–6
dress style 108, 125–6
Duelli-Klein, Renate 104
Dworkin, Andrea 145n.29

Eagleton, Terry 73
Eastern Europe
  femininity 124–6
  state and welfare 32, 33, 34
ecology 136
education 28, 33, 39, 42, 53
  see also academy
Ehrenreich, Barbara 31, 39, 98
Einhorn, Barbara 32
Eliot, George 72, 78
Ellmann, Mary 76
Engels, F. 11, 60
English, Deirdre 39, 98
English literature 112, 116
  see also literary criticism
Enlightenment 15, 16, 25, 27, 55
equality 138
essentialism 136, 137
ethnicity 12, 83
expert, critique of 19

Faderman, Lillian 87
family 24, 27, 30–1, 49
family planning 13
  see also contraception
Fawcett Society 16

164

Index

Fee, Elizabeth 57
feminine 39, 51, 54, 79–80, 86, 101, 108, 133–4
  Eastern Europe 124–6
  impossibility of representing 49
  Western/state socialist models of 124–8
feminism
  black 61–2, 83
  complexity/diversity 9
  early 9, 15, 16
  emergence of contemporary 12, 107
  fragmentation 12, 20, 62–3
  projects of early 1970s 11, 107
  second wave feminism 7–23, 44, 65, 84, 107, 109, 114
  and social and intellectual world 123–38
  white, middle-class values 8, 18, 99, 102, 135
  see also academy, feminism and; de-constructionist feminism; Marxist feminism
feminist networks 18, 111
Feminist Review 18, 101, 140n.17, 141n.21
Feminist Studies 114
feminist theory, rise of 17–23
fiction 61, 62
  feminist 10, 57–8, 68–9, 83
fictive/real 119, 134–5
films *see* cinema
Firestone, Shulamith 9, 15
Foucault, Michel 2, 20, 29, 35–6, 52, 80–1, 90–2, 100, 130, 131
Fox Keller, Evelyn 56, 57
France 7, 15, 18, 47–9, 68, 77, 114
Franklin, Rosalind 54
Freud, Anna 48
Freud, Sigmund 2, 22, 47, 48, 50, 51, 63, 66, 75, 79, 90, 91, 104, 115, 120–1, 130
Friedan, Betty 15, 60

Gardner, Katy 119–20
Gaskell, Mrs 72, 96
Gavron, Hannah 60
gay men 10, 21, 30, 52, 82, 87–8, 90, 100, 129, 130
gender 86
  institutions and 4, 29, 38–43
gender ambiguity 104
gender bending 108
gender difference 9, 16, 21, 32, 124, 131
  recognition/non-recognition of 32, 38, 107–9
gender divisions 56
gender identity 68, 103–4, 147n.29
gender politics 27, 68, 72
Gender Studies 13
Gibbons, Stella 75
Giddens, Anthony 131–2
Gilbert, Sandra 62, 76, 80
Gilligan, Carol 63
globalization 12, 135–6
Gordon, Linda 36, 61, 95
Graham, Hilary 36
grand narratives 46
Greenham Common 136
Greer, Germaine 9, 10, 15, 18, 69, 88, 89, 90, 93, 102
Grosz, Elizabeth 104, 110
Gubar, Susan 62, 76, 80

Hadley, Janet 33–4
Hall, Catherine 43, 122, 125
Hall, Stuart 66
Hanmer, Jalna 118
Haraway, Donna 54, 59, 136
Harding, Sandra 54–5, 58, 121–2
Hardwick, Elizabeth 73
Hartsock, Nancy 137
Harvey, David 141n.31
heterosexuality 5–6, 68, 78, 87
  literary criticism 82
  modern Western 128
  women and 10, 11, 21, 88, 90, 94, 98–100, 102
higher education *see* academy
Hill Collins, Patricia 144n.29
history 111
  feminist 52–6, 60, 95–7, 129
Hobsbawm, E.J. 131
Hoggart, Richard 66
Home, Evelyn 5
homophobia 130

homosexuality 68, 82, 87–8, 100
  see also gay men; lesbianism
hooks, bell 43
Horney, Karen 48
household *see* family
housework 14, 19, 60
humanities 19, 20, 106
Humm, Maggie 15, 83
Humphries, Jane 27

identity
  gender 68, 103–4, 147n.29
  politics of 131
  see also sexual identity; women,
    identity
imperialism 43, 62, 83
individualism 125, 135
international agencies 13
Iran 34
Irigaray, Luce 15, 47, 48, 49, 51, 52,
    56, 64, 104
Islam 34, 109

Jagger, Alison 63–4
Jardine, Alice 79
Jeffreys, Sheila 11, 15, 87, 100,
    139n.2
Johnston, Jill 10
Jong, Erica 10, 57, 68, 93
Jordanova, Ludmilla 56

Kaluzynska, Eva 18
Kaplan, Cora 74, 75, 76
Kelly, Mary 71
Kennedy, Jacqueline 125, 126,
    127
Khrushchev, Mrs 125–6
Kinsey, Alfred 92
Klein, Melanie 48
Klein, Viola 40
knowledge 107, 119, 133
  gendered 3, 44–63
Kohlberg, Lawrence 63
Komarovsky, Mirra 40
Kosofsky Sedgwick, Eve 82, 147n.29
Kristeva, Julia 22, 49, 50, 56, 64, 70,
    77, 78–9, 104
Kuhn, Annette 84
Kuhn, Thomas 133

Lacan, Jacques 22, 47, 48, 49, 50,
    77, 121
language 44, 47–9, 56, 64, 77–8
Larkin, Philip 5
law 16–17, 28, 33, 34, 36–9, 42, 87,
    118
Le Doeuff, Michelle 104
Leavis, F.R. 66
Leavis, Q.D. 66
lesbianism 10, 21, 30, 88, 89–90,
    92–3, 98–100, 102, 135
  see also radical feminism/lesbianism
literary criticism 57, 65–84
  see also individual fields of
Llewellyn Davies, Margaret 86
Lorde, Audré 2, 15, 43, 62
Lukács, Georg 66
Lynd, Robert 112

McDowell, Linda 43
McIntosh, Mary 29–30, 33, 36,
    93–4, 95, 141n.1
Macey, David 91
Mackinnon, Catherine 118
Madonna 126, 128
Madonnas/Magdalenes 17, 29, 33
male gaze 71, 82, 125
man, as category 104
  see also masculinity; men
market economy 118, 138
marriage 11, 70–1, 131
Marwick, Arthur 142n.12
Marx, Karl 2, 3, 11, 60, 130, 131
Marxism 11, 21, 36, 46
Marxist feminism 60
Marxist literary criticism 66
masculinity 39, 45–6, 67–8, 79–80,
    94, 104, 128–9
  values of, accepted as normality 4,
    13–14, 45, 46, 61, 135, 137
master narratives (Henrietta
    Moore) 134
materialism, and gender 132
materialist feminism 14, 60
media studies 3
medicine 28, 32, 36, 39, 41–2, 56,
    102, 118
  introduction of unisex to
    hospitals 108, 109

Index

reproductive technology 34, 104
men
  difference between worlds of men
    and women 123–38
  domination of academy 19–20, 46,
    53, 55, 56, 58, 110–14
  sexual desire 10, 93–4, 124
  social power 24–43, 132
  see also masculinity
military, feminism and 136, 137
Miller, Nancy 78
Millett, Kate 9, 10, 15, 18, 57, 58, 73,
  75, 88–9, 90, 92, 102, 140n.10
Mills, C.W. 19, 112
Mitchell, Juliet 15, 22, 47, 48, 91
modern/conservative perceptions of
  gender/sexual difference 108–10
modernism 67, 74, 78–9, 85–6
  sexual attitudes 97
modernity 12
Moers, Ellen 73, 76
Moi, Toril 74, 76–7
Molyneux, Maxine 32
Monroe, Marilyn 126
Moore, Henrietta 134, 142n.29
moral agency, art and literature 81,
  82
moral motherhood (Cott) 96–7
moral reasoning, gender and 63
Morgan, Robin 11, 52
Morrison, Toni 83
Moss, Kate 126
motherhood 99–100
  see also moral motherhood (Cott)
Munday, Diana 34

nationality 12, 43
nature, women and 39, 49–53, 55,
  59, 61, 63
New, Caroline 136–7
new men 132
Nietzsche, F. 110
North/South relations 12, 43, 127,
  136
Nussbawm, Martha 38

Oakley, Ann 14, 41, 60, 118
objectivity 1, 56–7, 67, 112, 119–20
O'Rourke, Rebecca 75

Orwell, George 67
Oxford University 112

pacifism 45
Paglia, Camille 129
Pahl, Jan 146n.7
Pateman, Carole 3
patriarchy 15, 16–17, 31, 32, 33, 34,
  36, 60, 73, 86, 107, 120–1
peace movement 124
personal appearance 108, 125–6
personal/political 6, 11
Phillips, Anne 141n.21
philosophy 63–4
Phizacklea, Annie 43
photography 71, 81
Pinchbeck, Ivy 58
Plath, Sylvia 84, 128, 129
pluralism 46, 66, 117
Poland, abortion in 33–4
political/personal 6, 11
politics
  of 1960s 6–7
  and academy 112–18 passim
  feminism and 2–3, 44–5
  women's supposed affiliations 4
  see also citizenship; sexual politics;
    state socialism; voting rights
popular culture 10, 66, 67, 83–4, 108
pornography 71, 81, 82, 101, 118
positivism, feminist literary
  criticism 76
post-modernity/post-
  modernism 20–1, 81, 82, 84, 85,
  117
post-structuralist literary criticism 74
power 17
  academy 1–3, 19–20, 107, 119
  heterosexual 21
  household and state 24–43
Price, Marion 41
private/public see public/private
professions, women and 28, 39, 40,
  41, 54, 55, 71, 111, 137
prostitution 93–4
Proust, Marcel 68, 78
psychoanalysis 22, 47–9, 50, 51, 105
  and feminist literary criticism 66,
  72, 74, 77

Index

psychology 59, 120
public/private 14, 19, 21, 24–43, 80, 86, 122
  and masculinity/femininity 127–30
publishing 18, 68, 71

queer theory 147n.29

race 6, 11, 12, 20, 43
  literature and 62, 83
racism 41, 43, 97
radical feminism/lesbianism 11, 51, 93, 99, 102
radicalism 2–3, 7, 99
rape 16–17, 33, 35, 37, 81, 94, 124
representation 21, 65–84
  of body 102
Rhys, Jean 62
Rich, Adrienne 15, 51–2, 98–100, 146n.22
Richardson, Henry 73
Right, the 30, 33
Roberts, Michèle 75
Roman Catholic Church 33–4
Rose, Hilary 54–5, 58
Rose, Jacqueline 48, 79, 84
Roseneil, Sasha 3
Rossi, Alice 54, 57
Rousseau, Jean-Jacques 26
Rowbotham, Sheila 8, 9, 15, 16, 18, 60
Rubin, Gayle 52, 101
Rubin, Lillian 146n.7
Ruskin College, Conference (1971) 14

Sayers, Dorothy 132–3
Sayers, Janet 48, 91, 140n.12
Sayre, Ann 54, 55
Schiebinger, Londa 39, 53–4, 55, 58
Schofield, Michael 92
science, gender and 39, 52–7, 58–9
Scott, Joan 60, 145n.27
second wave feminism 7–23, 44, 65, 84, 107, 109, 114
Second World War 40, 66
sex roles 22
sex/sexuality distinction 80–1, 100
sexism 32, 41, 43, 57, 71, 86

sexual ambiguity 79
sexual behaviour
  changes in 5–6, 10, 31, 87–8, 100–1
  diversity 21
sexual codes, Victorian 94–7
sexual desire 15, 47, 48, 80–1, 82, 93–4, 96, 102, 124
sexual difference 16, 21, 50, 56, 105, 109, 110, 115, 124, 136–7
sexual division 56
sexual division of labour 43, 59, 60, 131
sexual equality 35
sexual identity 22, 75, 78–9
sexual libertarianism 5, 7, 87, 88, 89, 126, 130
sexual morality 28, 87, 88
sexual pleasure 90–2
sexual politics 21, 37, 67, 76–7, 91, 92–3, 100
sexuality 52, 87–105
  distinct from sex 80–1, 100
Shelley, Mary 53
Showalter, Elaine 62, 73, 76, 77, 80
Signs 94–5, 98
Simmel, Georg 74
sisterhood 11, 12, 20, 89
Smart, Barry 93
Smart, Carol 37, 93
Smith-Rosenberg, Caroll 94–5, 96
social class *see* class
social constructionist feminism 136
social power, women and 24–43
social sciences 19, 20, 22, 106, 119
social theory 2
social worlds, of men/women 123–38
socialism, feminism and 140n.6
socialist feminist historians 60, 61
socialist literary criticism 69
socialization 50
sociology 52, 59, 111, 112, 116, 120, 131–2
Spence, Jo 71
Spender, Dale 47
Spivak, Gayatri Chakravorty 43, 62, 130
Spring-Rice, Margery 86

Index

Stacey, Jackie 84
Stacey, Margaret 41
standpoint, women's 58, 64, 121
Stanley, Liz 97, 119, 120
Stanworth, Michelle 104
state, women and 24–43
state socialism 32, 49
  and femininity 124–6
Stott, Rebecca 97
structuralism 21
student protest (1968) 6–7
subject/subjectivity 1, 13–14, 21, 120
  gendered 106
  literary 67, 78, 80, 86
Swingewood, Alan 144n.2
symbolic constructions 49, 50, 65,
  134

Tanner, Tony 79
Taylor, Barbara 27, 61, 141n.21
Tel Quel 49
Temkin, Jennifer 37
Thatcherism 118
theatre 71, 103
Thompson, E.P. 113
Tilly, Louise 144n.25
time, women's 70
Tolstoy, Leo 73, 78

unisex 108–9
United Nations 13
United States 6–7, 36, 43, 113, 118,
  126, 130
  abortion 33, 35
  feminism 8, 15, 57, 59, 61, 73, 75,
    76, 83, 94, 101, 137
  lesbianism 10, 102
  masculinity 68, 128–9
  sexuality 6, 92
  women's publishing 18
  women's writing 68–9, 83
universalism 3, 40, 44–5, 46, 62, 64,
  122, 134
universities see academy

Victorian sexual codes 94–7
Vietnam 6, 7, 45
Virago Modern Classics 18, 68, 69
virgins/whores 17, 29, 33

visual arts 65–84
voting rights 8, 25, 28, 40

Walby, Sylvia 140n.15, 141n.24
Walker, Alice 57, 83
Weeks, Jeffrey 87, 139n.2
welfare state/services 28–31, 36, 39,
  42
Western culture see culture
Western model of female
  emancipation 125–30
Western politics in 1960s 6–7
Williamson, Judith 84
Willmott, Peter 19
Wilson, Elizabeth 18, 74, 101, 108
Wise, Sue 119, 120
Wittig, Monique 47, 49, 51, 136
Wolfe, Tom 129
Wollstonecraft, Mary 9, 15, 26, 40,
  43, 53, 138
woman 13, 49, 104, 106, 110, 136
  in literary criticism 74–6
women
  arts, in 65–84
  autonomy 10, 16, 107–8, 110,
    125, 127, 132–3
  as carers/homemakers 14, 31, 32,
    33, 40, 59–60, 102
  differences between 11, 17, 20,
    62–3, 136
  exploitation/oppression of 11, 90,
    105, 124, 130; by women 89,
    102
  'good'/'bad' 16–17, 29, 33, 37,
    103, 136
  identity 110, 124
  social rights 8, 16; see also
    citizenship; voting rights; social
    power
  as victims/agents 35, 69, 73, 82
  violence against 33, 118, 131; see
    also rape
  see also heterosexuality, women
    and; nature, women and
women writers 75–6
  black 68–9, 83
  see also fiction
women's movement 21–2, 58, 89, 94,
  101, 116, 118

women's networks 18, 111
women's publishing 18, 68
Women's Studies 1, 13, 22, 59, 69,
     87, 95, 106–7, 111, 112, 114–18,
     119
Woolf, Janet 71, 72
Woolf, Virginia 45, 67, 72, 78, 79, 86
work 14, 21, 27, 28, 30–3, 40, 43, 104
  domestic 14, 19, 60

working class, in fiction 69
working-class women 8–9, 27, 29,
     36, 61
World Forum on Women, Beijing
     (1995) 126–7, 130

Young, Michael 19
Yugoslavia, former 124–5